Queer Theory

Queer Theory

An Introduction

Annamarie Jagose

NEW YORK UNIVERSITY PRESS
Washington Square, New York

Published in 1996 by Melbourne University Press

First published in the U.S.A. in 1996 by
NEW YORK UNIVERSITY PRESS
Washington Square
New York, N.Y.   10003
Reprinted 1997, 1998, 2000, 2001, 2002

CIP data available from the Library of Congress
ISBN 0-8147-4233-5 (clothbound)
ISBN 0-8147-4234-3 (paperbound)

Printed in Malaysia

Contents

The appeal of 'queer theory' has outstripped anyone's sense of what exactly it means.
Michael Warner

1

Introduction

Once the term 'queer' was, at best, slang for homosexual, at worst, a term of homophobic abuse. In recent years 'queer' has come to be used differently, sometimes as an umbrella term for a coalition of culturally marginal sexual self-identifications and at other times to describe a nascent theoretical model which has developed out of more traditional lesbian and gay studies. What is clear, even from this brief and partial account of its contemporary deployment, is that queer is very much a category in the process of formation. It is not simply that queer has yet to solidify and take on a more consistent profile, but rather that its definitional indeterminacy, its elasticity, is one of its constituent characteristics.

Given this situation, it may seem counter-intuitive, even futile, to produce an introductory account of the queer phenomenon. For part of queer's semantic clout, part of its political efficacy, depends on its resistance to definition, and the way in which it refuses to stake its claim, since 'the more it verges on becoming a normative academic discipline, the less queer "queer theory" can plausibly claim to be' (Halperin, 1995:113). Judith Butler (1994:21) likewise cautions that 'normalizing the queer would be, after all, its sad finish', and Lauren Berlant and Michael Warner point out that 'because almost everything that can be called queer theory has been radically anticipatory, trying to bring a world into being, any attempt to summarize it now will be violently partial' (1995:344). To attempt an overview of queer theory and to identify it as a significant school of thought, which those in pursuit of general knowledge should be familiar with, is to risk domesticating it, and fixing it in ways that queer theory resists fixing itself. However, this book does not attempt to stabilise the mobile field of queer identification. Instead, it maps that very mobility, and situates it within a history of sexual categories which have evolved over the last hundred years or so. While specifying the different political and theoretical work currently being carried out under the rubric of 'queer', this book assumes that queer is 'a zone of possibilities' (Edelman, 1994:114) always inflected by a sense of potentiality that it cannot yet quite articulate.

The rapid development and consolidation of lesbian and gay studies in universities in the 1990s is paralleled by an increasing deployment of the term 'queer'. As queer is unaligned with any specific identity category, it has the potential to be annexed profitably to any number of discussions. Like many critical treatments of queer, however, this study reads it largely in relation to the more stable, more recognisable, categories of 'lesbian' and 'gay'. In the history of disciplinary formations, lesbian and gay studies is itself a relatively recent construction, and queer theory can be seen as its latest institutional transformation. Not only are new journals launched which specialise in the interdisciplinary field of lesbian and gay studies, but periodicals with other concerns bring out special issues on queer theory. Specialist journals include the North American *GLQ: A Journal of Lesbian and Gay Studies*, first published in 1993, and the Australian *Critical InQueeries*, whose first issue came out in 1995. Non-specialist periodicals which have each devoted a whole issue to queer theory include *Sociological Theory* (Summer 1994), *Socialist Review* (vol. 22, no. 1, 1992) and *Social Text* (vol. 9, no. 4, 1991), while *differences: A Journal of Feminist Cultural Studies* brought out two queer issues in 1991 and 1994. *Media Information Australia* and *Meanjin* published queer issues in late 1995 and early 1996 respectively. Universities are not only beginning to offer courses in lesbian and gay theory, but many of these courses are organised around notions of queer. This 'queering' of lesbian and gay studies has been the subject of violent debate. Some claim that it radically erodes the last traces of an oppressive gender coherence, whereas others criticise its pan-sexuality as reactionary, even unfeminist.

While there is no critical consensus on the definitional limits of queer—indeterminacy being one of its widely promoted charms—its general outlines are frequently sketched and debated. Broadly speaking, queer describes those gestures or analytical models which dramatise incoherencies in the allegedly stable relations between chromosomal sex, gender and sexual desire. Resisting that model of stability—which claims heterosexuality as its origin, when it is more properly its effect—queer focuses on mismatches between sex, gender and desire. Institutionally, queer has been associated most prominently with lesbian and gay subjects, but its analytic framework also includes such topics as cross-dressing, hermaphroditism, gender ambiguity and gender-corrective surgery. Whether as transvestite performance or academic deconstruction, queer locates and exploits the incoherencies in those three terms which stabilise heterosexuality. Demonstrating the impossibility of any 'natural' sexuality, it calls into question even such apparently unproblematic terms as 'man' and 'woman'.

The recent intervention of this confrontational word 'queer' in altogether politer academic discourses suggests that traditional models have been ruptured. Yet its appearance also marks a continuity. Queer theory's debunking of stable sexes, genders and sexualities develops out of a specifically lesbian and gay reworking of the post-structuralist figuring of identity as a constellation of multiple and unstable positions. Queer is not always seen, however, as an acceptable elaboration of or shorthand for 'lesbian and gay'. Although many theorists welcome queer as 'another discursive horizon, another way of thinking the sexual' (de Lauretis, 1991:iv), others question its efficacy. The most commonly voiced anxieties are provoked by such issues as whether a generic masculinity may be reinstalled at the heart of the ostensibly gender-neutral queer; whether queer's transcendent disregard for dominant systems of gender fails to consider the material conditions of the west in the late twentieth century; whether queer simply replicates, with a kind of historical amnesia, the stances and demands of an earlier gay liberation; and whether, because its constituency is almost unlimited, queer includes identificatory categories whose politics are less progressive than those of the lesbian and gay populations with which they are aligned.

Whatever ambivalences structure queer, there is no doubt that its recent redeployment is making a substantial impact on lesbian and gay studies. Even the formidable 650-page *The Lesbian and Gay Studies Reader*—whose very title seems to take a stand against queer's recent expansion—closes its introduction with a justification which is less a defence than defensive:

> It was difficult to decide what to title this anthology. We have reluctantly chosen not to speak here and in our title of 'queer studies,' despite our own attachment to the term . . . our choice of 'lesbian/gay' indicates no wish on our part to make lesbian/ gay studies look less assertive, less unsettling, and less queer than it already does. (Abelove et al., 1993:xvii)

Sticking to their formulation of 'lesbian/gay studies', the editors nevertheless worry that this might seem a conservative gesture. In asserting their wish not to make 'lesbian/gay studies look . . . less queer than it already does', they suggest that the older formation is already queer. This is by no means an idiosyncratic move. Queer's contemporary proliferation is enabled, in part, by claims that it has always already significantly structured the anti-homophobic impulse. Queer's powerful refiguring of lesbian and gay studies is evident in the way in which it is able to install itself retrospectively at the heart of that project. Although queer theory's institutional growth is commonly associated with academic developments in the early 1990s, the tendency to date its moment of origin increasingly earlier suggests an ambivalent figuring of queer as not only a radically new conceptual model but also one already imbricated in and informing existing knowledges of sexuality. In introducing her collection of 'deviant readings', *Perversions*, Mandy Merck (1993:1) describes the book as 'begun in London in the late 1970s, an era of Queer Studies *avant la lettre*'. Wayne Koestenbaum (1993:18) similarly antedates queer when describing Bertha Harris's novel *Lover* as 'a vaudeville version of queer theory; presciently it explains everything theory has come laboriously to know since 1976'. On the back-cover blurb of the 1993 edition of Guy Hocquenghem's *Homosexual Desire*, Douglas Crimp argues that while the book was 'written over two decades ago, in the aftermath of May '68 and Stonewall', it 'may well be the first example of what we now call queer theory'.

In a movement simultaneously forwards and backwards, queer is designated as not only the evolutionary extension of a more conventional lesbian and gay studies but also its bent progenitor. This slippage is evidenced in the difference between the first and second editions of Eve Kosofsky Sedgwick's *Between Men: English Literature and Male Homosocial Desire*. First published in 1985, and reprinted in 1992 with a new preface, *Between Men* dramatises the evolution of an ambivalent but productive relation between gay and queer. The back cover of the 1992 edition reproduces accounts of the book which situate it within that critical field which its publication significantly consolidated. According to *Rolling Stone*, it is 'universally cited as the text that ignited gay studies', while the *Village Voice Literary Supplement* describes it as 'in many ways, the book that turned queer theory from a latent to a manifest discipline'. If queer and gay seem synonymous here, in her new preface Sedgwick dramatises a historical and disciplinary shift through the mobilising of these terms. She notes that, while 'a growing gay and lesbian studies movement already existed in American academia at the time [1985]', between then and 1992 there emerged a 'highly productive queer community whose explicit basis is the criss-crossing of the lines of identification and desire among genders, races and sexual definitions' (Sedgwick, 1992:x). Yet having identified queer as a new structure whose energy and effectiveness developed out of a more established lesbian and gay model, in her last sentence Sedgwick recasts this developmental narrative by situating queer as the source rather than the destination of lesbian and gay studies. 'The proliferation . . . of so much subsequent work in the field', she writes, 'has vastly more to say for the inveterate, gorgeous generativity, the speculative generosity, the daring, the permeability, and the activism that have long been lodged in the multiple histories of queer *reading*' (ibid.).

Rather than represent queer as unequivocally either progressive or reactionary, this book argues that it does not have any fixed value. Simplistic attempts to evaluate this new terminology and conceptual framework ignore the fact that, since the late nineteenth century, knowledge of homosexuality has always been structured by strenuously contested categories (see, for example, Chauncey, 1982). Nor is this kind of classificatory uncertainty characteristic only of an unenlightened and remote historical moment. Similar claims have been made more recently, and specifically in relation to gay and lesbian studies. 'With the recent transformation of gay and lesbian studies from an underground phenomenon to an exciting area of academic discourse', notes Marilyn Farwell (1992:165), 'has come a strange plague: definition'. *Queer Theory* examines the constitutive discourses of homosexuality developed in the last century in order to place queer in its historical context and surveys contemporary arguments both for and against this latest terminology. In deferring any final assessment of queer as a critical term, this book acknowledges that if queer lives up to its radical potential—and does not solidify as merely another acceptable (though oppositional) category—its ongoing evolutions cannot be anticipated: its future is—after all—the future.

Theorising Same-Sex Desire

What is homosexuality exactly?

Homosexuality is commonly and widely understood to describe sexual attraction for those of one's own sex. There does not seem to be anything problematic or uncertain in such a definition. Nevertheless, the theoretical enterprise of deciding exactly what constitutes homosexuality—or, more pragmatically, who is homosexual—is far from self-evident. While there is a certain population of men and women who may be described more or less unproblematically as homosexual, a number of ambiguous circumstances cast doubt on the precise delimitations of homosexuality as a descriptive category. For example, is the man who lives with his wife and children, but from time to time has casual or anonymous sex with other men, homosexual? Many men in this situation, when interviewed for the purposes of AIDS research, did not identify themselves as homosexual. One interviewee said of his sexual identity: 'It's not important to me. I do it with men on occasions. It's more important that I am married and love my life. . . . It's no one's business what I do on my odd afternoon off' (Bartos et al., 1993:27). Another interviewee rejected a gay identity more explicitly:

> I am also not really gay. Gay sex is something that I do 2–3 times a week. It amounts to so little of my time. If you were to add up the time I spend looking for and having sex with men it

would total 1–2 hours weekly. The rest of the time I am heterosexual, married, a family man. (ibid:29)

Is the woman who identifies herself as a lesbian but is currently
in a sexual relationship with a man homosexual (cf. Califia, 1983;
Clausen, 1990)? What sexual category describes a woman currently in a sexual relationship with a self-identified gay man
(Schramm-Evans, 1993)? Is it possible to be homosexual without
ever having had or intending to have sex? These questions become more complicated when worked across cultural or historical
variations which raise the issue of whether 'homosexuality' is a
constant term in radically different contexts. As David Halperin
(1990:46) asks:

Does the 'paederast,' the classical Greek adult, married male
who periodically enjoys sexually penetrating a male adolescent
share *the same sexuality* with the 'berdache,' the Native
American (Indian) adult male who from childhood has taken
on many aspects of a woman and is regularly penetrated by the
adult male to whom he has been married in a public and
socially sanctioned ceremony? Does the latter share *the same
sexuality* with the New Guinea tribesman and warrior who from
the ages of eight to fifteen has been orally inseminated on a
daily basis by older youths and who, after years of orally
inseminating his juniors, will be married to an adult woman and
have children of his own? Does any of these three persons
share *the same sexuality* with the modern homosexual? (original
emphasis)

To a certain extent, debates about what constitutes homosexuality can be understood in terms of the negotiation between
so-called essentialist and constructionist positions. Whereas essentialists regard identity as natural, fixed and innate, constructionists
assume identity is fluid, the effect of social conditioning and available cultural models for understanding oneself. 'Essentialists hold
that a person's sexual orientation is a culture-independent, objective and intrinsic property', writes Edward Stein (1992b:325),
'while social constructionists think it is culture-dependent, relational and, perhaps, not objective'. Essentialists assume that homo-

sexuality exists across time as a universal phenomenon which has a marginalised but continuous and coherent history of its own. Constructionists, by contrast, assume that because same-sex sex acts have different cultural meanings in different historical contexts, they are not identical across time and space. For example, constructionists would not assume that a man was lying or deceiving himself when saying, 'I'm not gay. If I was gay I would kiss the men I have sex with. I never kiss men' (Bartos et al., 1993:29). Rather, they would assume that different meanings can attach themselves to the same sexual acts; moreover, they would argue that 'identity' is not a demonstrably empirical category but the product of processes of identification. While essentialism and constructionism are most frequently understood as oppositional categories, it is important to remember that they have a more complicated relation to each other than this suggests. There are certain coincidences between them (Fuss, 1989:1–21) and they are not synonymous with other related binarisms such as determinism and voluntarism (Stein, 1992).

It is often assumed that essentialist understandings of homosexuality are conservative, if not reactionary, in their consequences, whereas constructionist understandings of homosexuality lend themselves to progressive or even radical strategies. However, it is more correct to say that the nature of a political intervention is not necessarily determined by the assumption of either position. The essentialist claim that some people are born homosexual has been used in anti-homophobic attempts to secure civil rights-based recognition for homosexuals; on the other hand, the constructionist view that homosexuality is somehow or other acquired has been aligned with homophobic attempts to suggest that homosexual orientations can and should be corrected. Combinations of the two positions are often held simultaneously by both homophobic and anti-homophobic groups.

Consider, as a recent example, the controversial founding of the Queensland-based International Heterosexual Foundation, which 'aims to promote heterosexuality as the only lifestyle for teenagers' (Gurvich, 1995:2). In explaining the need for such a foundation, a spokesperson, Mr Kris Pickering, has recourse to both essentialist and constructionist models of homosexuality: 'He said only a small percentage of homosexuals were genetic homosexuals, and most were psychological homosexuals who chose that lifestyle because of a bad experience with a member of the opposite sex, together with influential propaganda promoting homosexuality' (ibid.). The Victorian AIDS Council vigorously disagreed with the International Heterosexual Foundation's description of heterosexuals as 'real people' (ibid.). Yet a spokesperson, Mr Eric Timewell, likewise framed their opposition in both essentialist and constructionist ways: '"Beyond the age of 11, people's sexual preferences are pretty well decided whether they know it or not"' (ibid.). Whereas Timewell sees constructionist and essentialist models working sequentially in the sexual development of any individual, Pickering understands them to be operating simultaneously throughout the population: '"People can help themselves from becoming homosexual, except that very small percentage"' (ibid.). In opposing one another on this issue, each man uses a combination of essentialist and constructionist assumptions to make his point.

The invention of homosexuality

The constructionist position so widely taken up in recent lesbian and gay studies is frequently sourced to the work of the French historian Michel Foucault, although as early as 1968 Mary McIntosh was proposing that 'the homosexual should be seen as playing a social role rather than as having a condition' (1992:29). In what was to become an enormously influential text for an as yet unimaginable lesbian and gay studies—volume 1 of *The History of Sexuality*—Foucault provides a persuasive historical narrative about the formation of a modern homosexual identity.[1]

Taking a constructionist line, Foucault argues that homosexuality is necessarily a modern formation because, while there were previously same-sex sex acts, there was no corresponding category of identification. Provocatively furnishing an exact date for the invention of homosexuality, Foucault (1981:43) writes:

We must not forget that the psychological, psychiatric, medical category of homosexuality was constituted from the moment it was characterized—Westphal's famous article of 1870 on 'contrary sexual sensations' can stand as its date of birth—less by a type of sexual relations than by a certain quality of sexual sensibility, a certain way of inverting the masculine and feminine in oneself.

Foucault's argument is premised on his assertion that around 1870, and in various medical discourses, the notion of the homosexual as an identifiable type of person begins to emerge. No longer simply someone who participates in certain sexual acts, the homosexual begins to be defined fundamentally in terms of those very acts: 'The nineteenth-century homosexual became a personage, a past, a case history . . . Nothing that went into his total composition was unaffected by his sexuality' (ibid.). Foucault argues that although same-sex sex acts were condemned in both religious and civil law before 1870, they were regarded as temptations to which anyone might succumb. Sinful and illegal, those forbidden acts were not understood to constitute a certain kind of individual. After 1870 same-sex sex acts began to be read as evidence of a particular type of person about whom explanatory narratives began to be formed: 'The sodomite had been a temporary aberration; the homosexual was now a species' (ibid.).

Foucault's confident dating of the emergence of the homosexual as 'a species' is rhetorically impressive. However, there is no critical consensus on the historical circumstances that gave rise to the modern homosexual. In his 1982 book, *Homosexuality in Renaissance England*, Alan Bray suggests a much earlier date—the late seventeenth century—and for quite different reasons. Following Foucault, he argues that, as late as the mid-seventeenth century, there was nothing equivalent to the modern conception of homosexuality. 'To talk of an individual in this period as being or not being "a homosexual" is an anachronism and ruinously misleading', he writes. 'The temptation to debauchery, from which homosexuality was not clearly distinguished, was accepted as part of the common lot, be it never so abhorred' (Bray, 1988:16–17).

Instead Bray argues that the origins of modern homosexuality can be discerned only fifty years later, at the close of the seventeenth century, with the emergence of an urban homosexual subculture that sprang up around those 'molly houses [which] were scattered across the whole of the built-up area north of the

Thames' (ibid:84; see also Norton, 1992). Whether private dwellings or part of a tavern, molly houses were places where men with sexual interests in other men gathered, but not necessarily for sex. For although 'sex was the root of the matter . . . it was as likely to be expressed in drinking together, in flirting and gossip and in a circle of friends as in actual liaisons' (Bray, 1988:84). Places for procuring sex with other men had existed previously but they were not as coherent as the system of molly houses, which constituted a community within a community, a specifically homosexual culture. Homosexuality came to be understood as the grounds for community; on this basis, a recognisable—though small and discreet—culture began to develop, which had its own 'ways of dressing, of talking, distinctive gestures and distinctive acts with an understood meaning, its own jargon' (ibid.:86). The molly houses provided a cultural context for homosexual identity and community, in so far as they constituted a nascent homosexual subculture, which 'existed independently of the individuals who might compose it at any time', and was distinguishable from the surrounding culture (ibid). Bray argues that the molly houses are significant because they constituted homosexuality as more than a sexual act or inclination; in fact, they constituted it in the modern sense as an identity, a way of being in the world.

Like Foucault, John D'Emilio argues that it is the late nineteenth century which provides a significant context for the emergence of modern homosexuality. Whereas for Foucault the decisive event is an increasing medicalisation of sexuality in that period, D'Emilio (1992b:5) takes a Marxist approach and argues that what generates the conditions necessary for a homosexual identity is the 'historical development of capitalism—more specifically, its free-labor system'. In mapping the growth of capitalism in the United States, D'Emilio focuses on the ways in which the family or household became decreasingly self-sufficient in terms of its patterns of production and consumption. No longer primarily a self-contained economic system, the family came to be thought of as an affective unit, that is, as 'an institution that provided not goods but emotional satisfaction and happiness' (ibid.). Jeffrey Weeks (1977:2) makes a similar point in relation to the United Kingdom when arguing that the best way of understanding 'the emergence of new definitions of homosexuality and the homosexual' is to see them 'as part of the restructuring of the family and sexual relations consequent upon the triumph of urbanization and industrial capitalism'. For D'Emilio (1992b.:8), the same shifts that enabled heterosexuality to be invested culturally with meanings other than the procreative also created conditions for the emergence of urban homosexual communities:

> Only when individuals began to make their living through wage labor, instead of as parts of an interdependent family unit, was it possible for homosexual desire to coalesce into a personal identity—an identity based on the ability to remain outside the heterosexual family and to construct a personal life based on attraction to one's own sex.

All accounts of the invention of homosexuality considered so far deal with the formation of male homosexuality. This is partly because these theorists focus on male examples and partly because the formation of female homosexuality or lesbianism does not follow exactly the formation of male homosexuality. Female homosexuality does not occupy the same historic positions as male homosexuality in the discourses of law or medicine. For example, the internationally influential British judicial system—which during Britain's colonial period was adopted or enforced as the legal template in many other countries—criminalised male homosexual acts while ignoring the possibility of female homosexuality. The Labouchère Amendment of 1885, on which much current anti-homosexual western legislation is founded, specifically outlaws acts of 'gross indecency' between 'male persons', but leaves comparable acts between female persons legal by default. Similarly—and partly as a consequence of its different relation to criminalisation—female homosexuality took much longer than male homosexuality to constitute the basis of a communal, subcultural identity.

The most influential and detailed account of the development of the modern lesbian identity is Lillian Faderman's book, *Surpassing the Love of Men* (1985). Spanning the sixteenth to the twentieth centuries, Faderman reads a range of historical and literary texts in order to demonstrate the ubiquity in western culture of sexual or intensely affectionate relations between women. Before the twentieth century, she argues, romantic friendships between women—which may or may not have been sexual— were socially sanctioned. Neither declarations of intense and sensual affection between women nor pledges of eternal and faithful devotion were pathologised: 'There is nothing to suggest that [romantic friends] were self-conscious about these passions or saw them as being abnormal in any way' (Faderman, 1985:125). Even when sexual activity between women was written of disparagingly, 'lesbianism itself was seldom the focal point of attack', since the 'aggressive sexuality [of the lesbian] was used primarily as a metaphor' to reprimand women who behaved in 'an unwomanly fashion' (ibid:45–6).

Repeatedly, Faderman declares herself surprised at the absence of any social condemnation of female romantic friendships. Assuming that romantic friendships and lesbianism are historical variants of the same thing, Faderman asks: 'If these romantic friendships were in the quality and intensity of the emotions involved no different from lesbian love, why were they so readily condoned in earlier eras and persecuted in ours?' (ibid:19). What produced the change in attitude, she believes, were reactionary responses to the demands of first-wave feminism, and—even more emphatically—the increasing tendency by sexologists to pathologise female homosexuality:

> Love between women was metamorphosed into a freakishness, and it was claimed that only those who had such an abnormality would want to change their subordinate status in any way. Hence, the sexologists' theories frightened, or attempted to frighten, women away from feminism and from loving other women by demonstrating that both were abnormal and were generally linked together. (ibid:240)

Despite its fascination with the conditions that contributed to the formation of lesbian identity, Faderman's book is resolutely un-Foucauldian, and the more surprisingly so because it draws back from the Foucauldian conclusions its argument seems to invite. *Surpassing the Love of Men* considers the increasing medicalisation of *fin de siècle* romantic friendship as a devaluation of the lesbian identity, not as the moment of its modern formation. Despite this, Faderman's extensive research into the formation and proliferation of a twentieth-century lesbian identity as represented in sexology, literature and popular magazines can be seen to demonstrate not the pathologisation of an already existing model of identity but rather the articulation of a new—but demonised—sexual category.

More recently Valerie Traub has offered a constructionist account of the historical circumstances which enabled the development of a modern lesbian identity. In analysing some female–female erotic discourses produced before 1800, Traub argues that European colonial anthropology, travel narratives and anatomy texts persistently associated the clitoris with tribadism— 'an early modern antecedent to "lesbianism"'—and that this connection has 'haunted modern discourse ever since' (Traub, 1995:82, 94). Avoiding the essentialising argument of Faderman, Traub neither conflates tribadism with lesbianism nor imagines that her project is to locate 'a pre-Enlightenment "lesbian" identity' (ibid.:85). However, she argues that 'notwithstanding assumptions about the nonexistence or invisibility of "lesbians", a vocabulary was available to Western writers with which to describe women's erotic desire for and contact with each other' (ibid:88). Her purpose in specifying an early modern erotic desire between women is not to give substance to a recognisably lesbian identity but to 'demonstrate the conditions of emergence *for* such an identity' (ibid.:85).

Although theories concerning the formation of modern homosexuality differ, there is significant agreement that homosexuality, as it is understood today, is not a transhistorical phenomenon. With the exception of Faderman, all the theorists discussed so far make crucial the distinction between homosexual *behaviour*, which is ubiquitous, and homosexual *identity*, which evolves under specific historical conditions. As Jeffrey Weeks (1972:2) writes:

Homosexuality has existed throughout history, in all types of society, among all social classes and peoples, and it has survived qualified approval, indifference and the most vicious persecution. But what have varied enormously are the ways in which various societies have regarded homosexuality, the meanings they have attached to it, and how those who were engaged in homosexual activity viewed themselves.

Halperin (1990:46) draws out the cultural implications of the same argument when observing that 'although there are persons who seek sexual contact with other persons of the same sex in many different societies, only recently and only in some sectors of our society have such persons—or some portion of them—been homosexuals'.

Homosexuality and heterosexuality

To foreground only those processes that resulted historically in the formation of homosexuality is to imply that heterosexuality—that frequently unremarked but no less historically contingent category—is somehow the more self-evident, natural or stable construction. This assumption is naturalised in a culture that commonly understands homosexuality to be a derivative or less evolved form of heterosexuality. Such an understanding is voiced in a number of different discourses, ranging from popular psychology—which offers supposedly reassuring accounts of homosexuality as a stage through which adolescents pass before maturing into heterosexuals—to those religious and legal definitions of 'family' by which homosexual family groupings are declared illegitimate or inauthentic. Heterosexuality cannot be substantially investigated here but many theorists argue that recent definitions of homosexuality and accounts of its historic development have important implications for naturalised or common-sense understandings of heterosexuality. For example, many theorists argue that since the term 'heterosexuality' is a back formation of 'homosexuality'—the former circulating only after the latter—heterosexuality is derivative of homosexuality, and that such a genealogy has important ideological consequences (Katz, 1983:147–50). Although heterosexuality is too often represented as unremarkable, it is significant that what distinguishes the emergence of "the homosexual" during the second half of the nineteenth century is the fact that at this time it became inseparable from and literally incomprehensible without its "normal" twin, "the heterosexual"' (Cohen, 1993:211).[2]

Heterosexuality, then, is equally a construction whose meaning is dependent on changing cultural models. As a descriptive term its provenance is historical, no matter how often it lays claim to universality. It is difficult to think of 'homosexuality' not as a self-evidently descriptive term for certain identifications or inclinations but as a historically and culturally contingent category. It is even more difficult to think of 'heterosexuality' in this way on account of the extent to which it has been naturalised. Heterosexuality, after all, has long maintained its claim to be a natural, pure, and unproblematic state which requires no explanation. Indeed, in so far as many attempts to 'explain' homosexuality are grounded conceptually on heterosexuality, there is a sense in which heterosexuality is assumed to be a neutral or unmarked form of sexuality *per se*. In his account of late nineteenth-century understandings of same-sex desire as 'inversion', Christopher Craft (1989:223) argues that 'unable or unwilling to deconstruct the heterosexual norm, English accounts of sexual inversion indeed repeat it; desire remains, despite appearances, essentially and irrevocably heterosexual'.

In the late twentieth century both heterosexuality and, to a lesser extent, homosexuality have been thoroughly naturalised. This makes it difficult to think of either category as having histories, as being arbitrary or contingent. It is particularly hard to denaturalise something like sexuality, whose very claim to naturalisation is intimately connected with an individual sense of self, with the way in which each of us imagines our own sexuality to be primary, elemental and private. Halperin (1990:53) admits to just such an 'awkward spot' when, having argued for sexuality as a cultural construct, he closes by saying that heterosexuality and homosexuality

> aren't merely categories of thought ... they're equally categories of erotic response, and they therefore have a claim on my belief that's stronger than intellectual allegiance. That, after all, is what it means to be acculturated into a sexual system: the

conventions of the system acquire the self-confirming inner truth of 'nature.' If one could simply think oneself out of one's acculturation, it wouldn't be acculturation in the first place.

To denaturalise either homosexuality or heterosexuality is not to minimise the significance of those categories, but to ask that they be contextualised or historicised rather than assumed as natural, purely descriptive terms.

Phrases such as 'homosexuality in the modern sense' or 'homosexuality as it is understood today' effectively draw attention to the paradigm shift from sexual acts to sexual identities, and to the problems inherent in assuming continuity between current and historically remote same-sex sex acts. Unfortunately, however, such phrases imply that modern homosexuality, unlike its predecessors, is coherent, certain and known. Much is invested culturally in representing homosexuality as definitionally unproblematic, and in maintaining heterosexuality and homosexuality as radically and demonstrably distinct from one another. Yet modern knowledges about the categories of sexual identification are far from coherent. Eve Kosofsky Sedgwick draws attention to this tendency to cast present knowledges of homosexuality as fixed and certain in comparison with their confused and unstable antecedents. She argues that the lesbian and gay development of a Foucauldian perspective on historical forms of same-sex desire has tended to exempt current formations of homosexuality from a similarly defamiliarising scrutiny. 'The topos of "homosexuality as we know it today"', she observes, 'has provided a rhetorically necessary fulcrum point for the denaturalizing work on the past done by many historians' (1990:45).

In critiquing this tendency to represent contemporary homosexuality as somehow self-evident and unproblematic, Sedgwick draws attention to logical contradictions in current understandings of homosexuality. Far from cancelling each other out, these unacknowledged inconsistencies often appear simultaneously. Sedgwick's aim in *Epistemology of the Closet* is to specify—although not to resolve—those mutually contradictory conceptual models which constitute modern homosexuality. She describes these contradictions in the following way:

The first is the contradiction between seeing homo/hetero-sexual definition on the one hand as an issue of active import-ance primarily for a small, distinct, relatively fixed homosexual minority (what I refer to as a minoritising view), and seeing it on the other hand as an issue of continuing, determinative importance in the lives of people across the spectrum of sexu-alities (what I refer to as a universalising view). The second is the contradiction between seeing same-sex object choice on the one hand as a matter of liminality or transitivity between genders, and seeing it on the other hand as reflecting an im-pulse of separatism—though by no means necessarily political separatism—within each gender. (ibid.:1–2)

Sedgwick argues that 'the now chronic modern crisis of homo/heterosexual definition' is a consequence of these two irresolvable contradictions, which constitute twentieth-century understandings —both homophobic and anti-homophobic—of homosexuality and heterosexuality. The first contradiction—between minoritising and universalising views—centres on how the group designated 'homosexual' is delimited: whether homosexuality is the identity of a small and distinct section of the general population or whether the identities of ostensibly heterosexual people are equally determined by same-sex desire. The second contradiction is the one between transitivity and separatism as models for the gendering of homosexual desire: the former characterises same-sex desire as proceeding from the homosexual's liminal or borderline location between genders; the latter constitutes homo-sexuality as the epitome of gender itself. Sedgwick (ibid.:83–90) argues that these two radical contradictions exist in tandem and thus ensure the fundamental incoherence of modern constitutions of homosexuality.

To some extent, the crisis—epidemiological, governmental, activist—brought about by AIDS exemplifies the discursive inco-herence that structures understandings of modern sexualities. Uni-versalising versus minoritising conceptions of homosexuality can be seen in struggles over governmental and medical management of AIDS. Misrecognised initially—and persistently—as a 'gay disease', AIDS attracted the attention of previously indifferent government agencies in North America only when it was perceived to be affecting what was callously referred to as 'the general population'.[3]

Activists were angered by the treatment of AIDS and homosexuality as discursively synonymous and concerned that such a metonymic slippage hampered effective intervention. They urged that the circuits of HIV transmission should be rethought, not in terms of minoritised and so-called 'risk groups'—gay men primarily, and other populations such as intravenous drug users and prostitutes—but with respect to universalised 'risk practices' like unsafe sex and the sharing of needles.

The importance of separating the concepts of homosexual identity and same-sex sex acts can be seen in recent health-policy reports, which emphasise both the urgency and the difficulty of targeting safe-sex information at men who have sex with other men but do not identify themselves as gay. As Gary Dowsett (1991:6–7) argues:

> MSM [men who have sex with men but who are unattached to gay communities] are not *a target group*. They cannot be clustered by demographic descriptors as has been done with gay men . . . They are UNgroupable in any way which might have previously been thought of as high-risk groups . . . The only thing they have in common—the experience of sex with their own sex—is not even shared in common; they have no culture of sexuality, such as that of gay men, in which to enjoy a sense of belonging. (original emphasis)

Acknowledging the phenomenon Dowsett describes, AIDS education programmes now commonly privilege acts over identities. Even this brief example of AIDS-education strategies demonstrates the limits of that paradigm shift which is widely understood to distinguish modern from premodern sexualities.[4] For in opposing the popular conflation of AIDS and homosexuality, such attempts at refiguring the discursive field of AIDS by emphasising acts rather than identities are more consonant with ancient laws than with that new regime which, for Foucault and his many adherents, inaugurates the modern.

Separatist versus transitive understandings of homosexual desire are also thrown into relief by popular knowledges about AIDS. Historically, the circumstantial development of the epidemic has resulted in gay male communities—among others—being devastated by AIDS. Yet for some there is a persistent association between lesbians and AIDS. Despite the fact that even now there is no accurate information about whether or how HIV is sexually transmitted between women (O'Sullivan and Parmar, 1989), transitive understandings of homosexuality continue to link lesbianism with AIDS. This conflation has not only prevented members of an American lesbian motorcycle club from making donations to a blood bank (on the grounds that their blood is unsuitable) but has also resulted in a political leader nominating 'gays, lesbians, and prostitutes [as] the source of AIDS' (Castle, 1993:12).

The discourse of AIDS here offers a contemporary instance of the long-standing definitional incoherence of homosexuality. In terms of Sedgwick's argument, it is not a matter of determining what homosexuality or heterosexuality really 'is', but of understanding that—despite various attempts (for a range of strategic purposes) to fix the definition of homosexuality—modern knowledges of it are structured by irresolvable incoherences and discontinuities.

It is evident that different understandings of homosexuality are mobilised in the early homophile movement, gay liberation, lesbian feminism and queer theory. Different historical circumstances and widely disparate models of knowledge have meant that no unbroken line can be traced between successive theoretical models and political strategies developed in relation to same-sex desire during the last century or so. What is sometimes less evident are certain relations of continuity that can be established productively between these different movements, each of which commonly represented itself as radically opposed to the configuration it succeeded. The following four chapters briefly discuss in turn the homophile movement, gay liberation, lesbian feminism and the ethnic model of gay identity in order to establish the specific cultural contexts in which queer has emerged as a contentious but significant critical term.

3

The Homophile Movement

It is difficult to specify with any accuracy the historical origin of anything as nebulous as the gay liberation and lesbian feminist movements. The following account of early homophile organisations surveys the larger contexts which brought about the rise of each. Gay liberation rhetoric commonly represents the distinction between homophile and liberationist movements as a clean break. Yet a close attention to the homophile movement enables a more historically nuanced understanding not only of the gay liberation and lesbian feminist movements but also of the political positions they advanced in common (D'Emilio, 1983), and their increasingly different priorities, necessitating their independent development.

While not becoming mass movements like gay liberation and lesbian feminism, homophile organisations set up educational programmes and worked towards political reform designed to increase tolerance of homosexuality and, in some cases, to decriminalise it. Originating in Europe—and particularly in Germany—at the end of the nineteenth century, they fought to have homosexuality recognised as a natural human phenomenon (Lauritsen and Thorstad, 1974). It is no accident that the homophile movements originate in the same period in which homosexuality crystallised as an identity, when for the first time it was possible to *be* a homosexual. For while homosexual behaviour had been subject to religious condemnation and legal prosecution for centuries, organised protest against such institutionalised prejudices was largely a consequence of the emergent identificatory category of 'homosexual'.

In 1869, when German legislators were considering a new penal code that would criminalise same-sex sex acts between men, Karoly Maria Benkert wrote an open letter to the minister of justice in opposition to the proposed legislation. His arguments anticipated and set part of the agenda for subsequent homophile interventions, and their timing has prompted the transhistorical argument that '1969 marks a rebirth, an anniversary—indeed, one might say the 100th anniversary of gay liberation' (Lauritsen and Thorstad, 1974:5). Benkert argued that, because homosexuality is innate, it can be subject only to the laws of nature, not penal law. He observed that homosexuality neither harmed anybody nor infringed their rights. In order to demonstrate the valuable contributions made to society and culture by 'homosexuals', he listed famous ones from different historical periods—Napoleon, Frederick the Great, Michelangelo, Shakespeare and Byron.

In 1897 a German neurologist called Magnus Hirschfeld founded the Scientific Humanitarian Committee. Its primary aim was to persuade the relevant legislative bodies to abolish Paragraph 175 of the penal code, which Benkert had opposed in his open letter, but which became law in 1871. Like Benkert, Hirschfeld emphasised the congenital nature of homosexuality. Developing Karl Ulrich's model, he understood homosexuality to be an intermediate condition, a 'third sex' that combined physiological aspects of both masculinity and femininity. The Scientific Humanitarian Committee emphasised both the harmless nature of homosexuality and the needless suffering caused by its criminalisation. Another important homophile group, founded by Benedict Friedländer five years after the Scientific Humanitarian Committee, was the Community of the Special. Although it supported Hirschfeld's petition campaign, it increasingly opposed the representation of homosexuality as a biological disposition. Friëdlander criticised Hirschfeld's conservative position as both 'degrading and a beggarly . . . pleading for sympathy', and he was openly scornful of the transitive idea of 'a poor womanly soul languishing away in a man's body, and of the third sex' (quoted in Lauritsen and Thorstad, 1974:50).

In 1914 the British Society for the Study of Sex Psychology was founded by the sexologists Havelock Ellis and Edward Carpenter. It had some connections with the German homophile groups, for example it reprinted one of the Scientific Humanitarian Committee's pamphlets on 'the third sex'. Yet the British group did not have the legislative focus of the Germans. 'We do not think', they declared, 'the time has yet arrived in England for a similar demand to be made' (quoted in ibid.:34). Ellis and Carpenter concentrated their energies accordingly on educational rather than legislative programmes, founded a library and made contacts with sympathetic people in the United States.[1]

The 1924 charter of the Chicago Society for Human Rights, which is the earliest recorded American homophile organisation, demonstrates similarly conservative tendencies when declaring its intention

> to promote and to protect the interests of people who by reasons of mental and psychic abnormalities are abused and hindered in the legal pursuit of happiness which is guaranteed them by the Declaration of Independence, and to combat the public prejudices against them by dissemination of facts according to modern science among intellectuals of mature age. The Society stands only for law and order; it is in harmony with any and all general laws insofar as they protect the rights of others, and does in no manner recommend any acts in violation of present laws nor advocate any matter inimical to the public welfare. (Katz, 1976:385)

In admitting that homosexuals have 'mental and psychic abnormalities', invoking the Declaration of Independence, upholding 'any and all general laws', and appealing to rationality in the form of 'modern science', the Chicago Society for Human Rights provided a template for later homophile organisations like the Mattachine Society and Daughters of Bilitis, which were founded in 1951 and 1955 respectively (D'Emilio, 1983).

Initially the Mattachine Society was almost a secret society. Organised as a number of cell groups that did not necessarily know one another, it was loosely structured like the Communist party, in which several of its founders had been active. Following a Marxist analysis of class oppression, early discussion papers theorised homosexuals as a population unaware of its status as 'a social minority imprisoned within a dominant culture' (quoted in ibid.:65). The Mattachine Society's political task was to foster a collective identity among homosexuals who, recognising the institutional and hegemonic investments in their continued marginalisation, might consequently be energised and enabled to fight against their oppression. Largely by word of mouth, the founding members established groups for men and women interested in talking about homosexuality, its place in American society and what caused it. There was also a sharing of personal experiences. As one participant in those discussion groups recalls, 'Just the freedom to open up . . . really, that's what it was all about. We had found a sense of belonging, of camaraderie, of openness in an atmosphere of tension and distrust' (quoted in ibid.:68).

Gradually the Mattachine Society branched out from its Los Angeles base to form groups in New York and Chicago as well as in other parts of California. In 1953 members of the Society launched the first issue of *One*, a homosexual magazine which displayed a 'combative pride in being gay' (ibid.:88) and, although not officially associated with the Mattachine Society, was largely produced by its members. The more accessible and public the Society became, the more problematic were its Communist origins. Many members of the Mattachine Society no longer knew or had even met its founders; in the 1950s, when the United States was dominated by McCarthyism, many new members were profoundly discomforted by their Society's historical links with the Communist party. Consequently, at a conference in May 1953, the Society rearticulated itself as a public organisation with by-laws, a constitution and democratically elected officers.

In the process of drawing up a constitution and determining future directions for the Society, two different groups emerged, one of which may be characterised as the founders and the other as their opposition. While the founders defended the rights of the Communist party to exist, their opponents spoke against the threat of Communist infiltration, and proposed that members of the Society should take a loyalty oath. The founders continued to represent homosexuals as a minority group oppressed by the dominant culture. Their opponents, however, advocated an assimilationist line, insisting that homosexuals were people like everyone else and that it was more productive for them to co-operate with experts in the fields of medicine, law and education in order to effect change. Although the founders won every point put to the vote, they decided not to stand for election. Consequently, the elected positions went to the organised opposition, and the Mattachine Society changed dramatically: 'accommodation to social norms replaced the affirmation of a distinctive gay identity, collective effort gave way to individual action, and confidence in the ability of gay men and lesbians to interpret their own experience yielded to the wisdom of experts' (ibid.:81). In ways that again emphasise the similarities rather than the differences between homophile and liberation movements, the political development of the Mattachine Society anticipated the mainstreaming of a later gay liberation.

Although avowedly interested in a gender-neutral homosexuality, the Mattachine Society was a masculinist organisation. Founded by men, it had a largely male membership which tended to perpetuate its predominantly male constituency through informal recruitment. It frequently focussed on issues not directly relevant to lesbians, such as the police entrapment of gay men. As D'Emilio observes: 'In numerous, often unconscious ways, male homosexuals defined gayness in terms that negated the experience of lesbians and conspired to keep them out of the Mattachine Society' (ibid.: 92–3). The uniquely homosexual identity and culture fostered by the Society's ¨founders was unequivocally masculine and even when restructuring itself the Society did not consider the issue of lesbian representation. The pressures of gender on the formation of a homosexual identity were not recognised as being either substantial or significant.

The Daughters of Bilitis redressed this situation. Founded originally by four lesbian couples as a social club that would provide an alternative to the lesbian bars of the 1950s, Daughters of Bilitis soon changed its priorities and became a political group committed to transforming dominant concepts of lesbianism. In 1956 Daughters of Bilitis began publishing a magazine, *Ladder*, which dealt with various issues, including maternity, lesbians in heterosexual marriages and employment. While associating itself with the Mattachine Society, Daughters of Bilitis maintained its specific interest in the circumstances of lesbians. In formal recognition of both the importance of gender issues and how easily they were disregarded by the Mattachine Society, an anti-amalgamation clause was written into the Daughters of Bilitis's constitution. Despite this, Daughters of Bilitis was regularly asked at joint events to defend the need for a separate women's organisation.

Set up as an alternative to—one might almost say in opposition to—the established subculture of predominantly working-class lesbian bars, Daughters of Bilitis disapproved of the visibly butch stylings of that culture, and its association with menial factory work. They advocated instead a more assimilationist set of values, recommending that lesbians dress in recognisably feminine ways in order to increase their chances of better paid employment. Daughters of Bilitis did not attract those lesbians who found support in the network of lesbian bars. Nor was it successful in securing the membership of lesbians already established in the professions, who did not need the kind of pastoral care and advice offered by Daughters of Bilitis, and whose continuing success depended on their lesbianism remaining a secret.

Although the Mattachine Society and Daughters of Bilitis often disagreed in their analyses of gender, they held very similar views on the transformation of public attitudes to homosexuality. By the late 1950s they concentrated on circulating information about homosexuality in magazines, newsletters and broadsheets. The conservative turn of these early homophile organisations can be seen in the fact that they now advertised themselves as organisations not for homosexuals but for those interested in homosexuality. Fearing any association with procurement or prostitution, they frequently denied there was any social dimension to what they called their fund-raising events. Moreover, they publicly dissociated themselves from anyone who transgressed received notions of gender propriety, such as drag queens or even butch women (Katz, 1976:406–33).

At times homophile organisations even represented homosexuals as abnormal, arguing that since homosexuality is a congenital condition, they deserved pity rather than persecution. The most famous literary example of this position is Radclyffe Hall's *The Well of Loneliness*, published in England in 1928. Hall's lover,

Una Troubridge, recalls the political intentions of this work on 'sexual inversion': 'It was [Hall's] absolute conviction that such a book could only be written by a sexual invert, who alone could be qualified by personal knowledge and experience to speak on behalf of a misunderstood and misjudged minority' (Troubridge, 1973:80). Although modern readers find the close of this tragic novel laughably overwrought, its demand for recognition and its plea for tolerance couched in—here religious—respectability is a recognisable strategy of later homophile organisations: '"God," she gasped, "we believe; we have told You we believe . . . We have not denied You, then rise up and defend us. Acknowledge us, oh God, before the whole world. Give us also the right to existence!"' (Hall, 1968:509). Homophile organisations sought the opinion of experts on the homosexual 'condition', and sent their materials even to those who considered homosexuality a disease. D'Emilio (1983:116–17) records that a San Francisco chapter of Daughters of Bilitis was addressed by a therapist who told them that, because it is the biological function of women to reproduce, lesbians can only lead unsatisfactory lives, and the Mattachine Society invited to one of its New York meetings a prestigious psychoanalyst who was renowned for characterising homosexuality as a disease. So entrenched was this habit of deferring to 'expert' opinion that when American homophile organisations argued in 1961 that there was no medical or scientific proof that homosexuality is a sickness, 'many movement people disputed [this], saying "We have to leave that up to the experts"' (Katz, 1976:427).

Neither the Mattachine Society nor Daughters of Bilitis ever became mass movements. Fear of the repercussions from being identified as homosexual in the 1950s meant that political organisation was difficult; even seemingly simple tasks, like publicising events or finding a mailing address for the organisation, were fraught with difficulty. Deference to the authority of professionals was problematic, and compromises to enable potential alliances with sympathetic heterosexuals were often made at the expense of developing a supportive homosexual milieu. The more established Mattachine Society, with its masculinist priorities and principles of organisation, did not encourage female membership. The Daughters of Bilitis failed to attract larger numbers of women partly because of the class prejudice that shaped its programme for reform. By 1960 there were only 230 members in the Mattachine Society, and 110 in Daughters of Bilitis. These figures indicate just how impossible it was for the homophile movement to succeed in 'appearing respectable to a society that defined homosexuality as beyond respectability' (D'Emilio, 1983:125).

From the vantage point of the 1990s it is easy to criticise the conventionality and conservatism of the homophile movement. This is why it is important to remember that the cultural conditions of the time largely determined the nature of possible resistance. For example, the mild-mannered Chicago Society for Human Rights was disbanded in 1925, only one year after its establishment, when police arrested key members without warrants and on such little 'evidence' as the alleged finding of a powder-puff in the secretary's bedroom (Katz, 1976:391). Moreover, the criticism that homophile organisations were not progressive enough has been enabled in part by the ground-breaking work undertaken in those early years.

Despite the limited achievements of these early homophile organisations, many of their political strategies are recognisable in the activities of more recent pressure groups. They petitioned governments, and sought statements from political candidates in periods leading up to elections; they published and distributed political newsletters and pamphlets; and they conducted 'large-scale statistical inquiries into homosexual behaviour' (Lauritsen and Thorstad, 1974:23). Although the similarities between homophile and liberationist movements are usually disavowed, some commentators have drawn attention to such continuities. 'The homophile movement', writes D'Emilio (1983:3), 'targeted the same groups and institutions as would gay liberation members in the 1970s—urban police forces, the federal government, the churches, the medical profession, the press and other media'. Retrospectively, there is a tendency to characterise the homophile movement as conservative rather than revolutionary, and therefore as the antithesis of gay liberation. It is worth remembering that in its radical origins it raised issues similar to those championed by gay liberation, but in a different context and with different effects.

4

Gay Liberation

On 27 June 1969 police who raided a New York gay and drag bar called the Stonewall Inn met with resistance, which culminated in a weekend of riots. A memorial service for Judy Garland—a long-established camp icon for many gay men—had been held earlier the same day. Commentators have described Stonewall dramatically as 'the shot heard round the homosexual world' (Cruikshank, 1982:69) or more campily in the New York Mattachine newsletter as 'The Hairpin Drop Heard Round the World' (D'Emilio, 1983:232). The twenty-seventh of June continues to be commemorated internationally—most enthusiastically in the United States —as Stonewall Day, a date which marks the constitution of lesbian and gay identities as a political force. Stonewall functions in a symbolic register as a convenient if somewhat spurious marker of an important cultural shift away from assimilationist policies and quietist tactics, a significant if mythological date for the origin of the gay liberation movement.

Among certain sections of the homosexual community in the late 1960s there was a growing dissatisfaction about the quietist position assumed by many groups dedicated to improving conditions for homosexuals. While still seeking legal and social recognition on the same terms as heterosexuals, homophile organisations were committed to securing this gradually, by means of persuasive rather than militant techniques. They argued that, apart from their same-sex sexual preferences, they were model citizens, as respectable as heterosexuals, and no more likely to disturb the status quo. No longer content to solicit tolerance and acceptance, more radical groups began to model themselves on New Left social movements and to critique the structures and values of heterosexual dominance. Instead of representing themselves as being just like heterosexuals except in their sexual object choice, gay liberationists—as they came to call themselves—challenged conventional knowledge about such matters as gendered behaviour, monogamy and the sanctity of the law. Regina Kahey (1976:94) describes this change in attitude: 'Lesbians and gay men are rapidly replacing *mea culpa* with "stick it in your ear"'. This new 'stick it in your ear' attitude was epitomised in the Stonewall riots. After all, what distinguished this now historical date was not that the police raided a known gay bar—for such occurrences were commonplace—but that the patrons resisted, many of them shouting proto-gay liberationist slogans at the police.[1]

Stonewall did not literally initiate the movement which came to be known as gay liberation. Yet its fortuitous and dramatic illustration of a break with homophile politics often causes it to stand in as the origin of the gay liberation movement. What characteristics can be discerned in those three-day riots at the Stonewall Inn, when acquiescence to authority gave way to resistance? They took place at a cultural site—a gay bar on Christopher Street frequented by drag queens and transvestites—that was both disreputable and an index of a nascent gay culture. They articulated notions of self-determination. They were militant in their expression of political disquiet. Whereas homophile organisations had called for a liberal approach to social change, gay liberation challenged the status quo. Homophiles favoured the improvement of public relations and presented images of homosexuality that would be acceptable to mainstream society. Gay liberationists, by contrast, refused to pander to heterosexual anxieties and scandalised society with their difference rather than wooing it with claims of sameness. Whereas the homophile movement had come to advocate assimilation, gay liberation was constructed around the notion of a distinctly gay identity. Although there were clearly significant lines of continuity between the two formations, 'essentially, however, gay liberation, to a much greater extent than is true of the older homophile groups, is concerned with the assertion and creation of a new sense of identity, one based on pride in being gay' (Altman, 1972:109). This is an important distinction and crucial to any understanding of the queer turn in lesbian and gay politics. It is precisely that 'new sense of identity'—and indeed that 'pride'—which became problematic in queer theory. In its impatience with gay liberationist ideals, queer rehearses with a difference some of the conflicts that gay liberation formerly had with the homophile movement.

Stonewall is located securely as the mythical origin of gay liberation. Yet the impetus to consolidate a mass movement—by developing a coherent sense of sexual politics and mobilising around newly politicised identities—requires a more substantial explanatory framework than a police raid on a gay bar. In spite of its conservatism, the homophile movement did much to generate an emergent sense of community and identity politics; although its attempts to transform itself into a mass movement were un-successful, its legacy benefited gay liberation. The history of the homophile movement demonstrates that oppression alone will not automatically politicise sexual identities. As Jeffrey Weeks (1985:191) remarks:

> they need complex social and political conditions for their emergence—to produce a sense of community experience which makes for collective endeavour. Five conditions seem to be necessary for this: the existence of large numbers in the same situation; geographical concentration; identifiable targets of opposition; sudden events or changes in social position; and an intellectual leadership with readily understood goals.

All of these conditions were met in the United States by the coalition of radical movements that constituted the New Left and provided much of the impetus for gay liberation. 'The Stonewall riot', according to D'Emilio (1983:233), 'was able to spark a nation-wide grassroots "liberation" effort among gay men and women in large part because of the radical movements that had so inflamed much of American youth during the 1960s'. It is not simply the fact that the men and women in the homophile movement were more conservative than those who were to constitute gay liberation. The social contexts of the two movements were also significantly different.

The counter-culture movement is an important context for gay liberation. 'By the late 1960s', writes D'Emilio (ibid.), 'a distinctively new culture of protest had taken shape in the United States, with which the reform orientation of the gay movement contrasted oddly'. Black militants, student radicals, hippies and anti-war activists were employing confrontational tactics in the form of street battles with police, bomb attacks, and the take-over of university buildings; meanwhile, the homophile movement was continuing to work for transformation through rational discussion and persuasion. The effect of counter-cultural movements on gay liberation was not limited to the United States, although that was their primary context. In his historical account of Sydney's gay subculture, Garry Wotherspoon (1991) similarly identifies 'ideas arising out of the counter-cultural revolution and the sexual liberation movement' as a critical factor in converting the city's gay sub-cultural groups to gay liberation. In many western countries, the success and proliferation of the counter-cultural movements enabled gay liberation to emerge by providing new models of organisational structure, ethical and ideological stances, and practices of resistance.

In his book *Homosexual Oppression and Liberation* (1972), Dennis Altman discusses the relations between American gay liberation and the other counter-cultural challenges to dominant culture. He argues that 'the critique of American society that gay liberation has adopted bears the marks of a decade of rising expectations and rising frustrations' (Altman, 1972:174). In particular, he singles out the black liberation (rather than the civil rights) movement, the women's movement and the youth revolt, which saw many 'turn on, tune in, drop out', partly in response to American involvement in Vietnam. Although not always committed to the same causes or principles, these different counter-cultural movements were unified in their opposition to the dominant culture. They criticised the unexamined grounds of the 'great American dream', with its ethos of hard work, individualism and family values. Altman argues that these various movements created a 'new consciousness', a suspicion of hypocrisy and a strong distrust of authority (ibid.:171). Initially gay liberation understood its own goals to mesh with those of other social movements and assumed that the different liberationist struggles of the counter-culture were connected. At times these links were formulated simplistically: 'Chick equals nigger equals queer. Think it over' (Wittman, 1992:332). Nevertheless, they indicated that gay liberation was not a single-issue struggle and that it could make sense only within an analytic framework capable of dealing with different forms of oppression. 'Gay liberation', writes Allen Young (1992:25–6), 'also has a perspective for revolution based on the unity of all oppressed people—that is, there can be no freedom for gays in a society which enslaves others through male supremacy, racism and economic exploitation (capitalism)'. As was clear from its rhetoric, political analysis and favoured strategies, the new form of gay liberation was an effect not only of the limitations of homophile politics but also of a new cluster of cultural movements, which collectively articulated a formidable critique of centralised power and dominant ideologies.

The overwhelmingly American slant to this account indicates the extent to which political developments in North America were influential—and, to a large extent, continue to be—in the development internationally of post-World War II gay and lesbian activism and analysis. As Altman (1982:217) was to remark, 'there is no doubt that if we can speak of the homosexualization of America, we can also speak of the Americanization of the gay world elsewhere'. Although he is critical of North American indifference to the local specificities of lesbian and gay initiatives in other countries, Altman nevertheless acknowledges that, because of 'the centrality of the United States in the world', the gay and lesbian movements internationally will continue to respond to parallel developments in America (Altman, 1990:64). Despite making a case for the local particularities of an Australian gay liberation movement, Altman (ibid.:63) concedes, somewhat hyperbolically, that

the United States occupies a special place in the imagination and fantasies of lesbians and gay men around the world. Castro Street, West Hollywood, and Fire Island (and, for women, the

Michigan Women's Music Festival, as well) are for us what Berlin and Paris were for American homosexuals between the wars.

Australian accounts of the rise of gay liberation frequently explain it in the context of American conditions: for example, Wotherspoon (1991) details the Cold War, second-wave feminism, the anti-war movement and the sexual revolution as crucial to the development of an Australian gay liberation (cf. Thompson, 1985). The American influence on gay liberation in other countries is often narrativised explicitly: 'Gay liberation arrived in London in 1970', according to Barry D. Adam (1987:83), 'when Aubrey Walter and Bob Mellors returned from New York to call a gay liberation meeting at the London School of Economics'. This phenomenon cannot be understood simply as the effect of American cultural imperialism, although that claim is made frequently. It is symptomatic of the perhaps overdetermined but undeniable ways in which, in the second half of the twentieth century, the United States has influenced many spheres of western life, ranging from systems of government, economic developments, international trade and peace agreements to forms of popular culture, vernacular expressions and subcultural style.

Far from being unimportant, local variations usefully identify those specific pressures and conditions that enable a more nuanced account of the international scope of gay liberation. Much interesting work has been undertaken in this area. Comparisons between American and Australian gay liberation have to take into account that in Australia there was nothing equivalent to the homophile movement. 'Unlike Britain, America, or Germany', notes Wotherspoon (1991:162), 'Australia had no prior history of gay activism': indeed, it was not until 1970 that a division of the American homophile group, Daughters of Bilitis, was formed in Melbourne as the Australian Lesbian Movement (ibid.:168). Denise Thompson's study of the nascent gay movement in Sydney in the 1970s notes that, precisely because 'there was no equivalent in Australia of the long-established [homophile] groups in the United States', the origins of the Australian gay movement differed from those of the American (Thompson,

1985:9). Organisers of the early group Campaign Against Moral Persecution (CAMP)

> were opposed to jumping on the American bandwagon in the wake of the 'Stonewall Riot'. They insisted that an Australian homosexual movement arose in a specifically Australian context. While they had no particular objection to the term 'gay' . . . they saw no reason why an Australian movement should automatically follow patterns set elsewhere, in response to different conditions. (ibid.)

In his preface to the 1978 edition of Guy Hocquenghem's *Homosexual Desire* (1972), Jeffrey Weeks discusses the different genealogy of gay liberation in France, given the French intellectual commitment to psychoanalysis and the fact that, under the Napoleonic legal code, homosexuality was not criminalised until 1942 (Hocquenghem, 1993:23–47). Barry D. Adam (1987: 82–9) surveys the geopolitical and socio-economic differences in different countries to explain variations in the gay liberatory models deployed in England, Canada, Australia, New Zealand, Germany, the Netherlands, France and Latin America. Notwithstanding its international proliferation, gay liberation often has a recognisably American spin, particularly in English-speaking countries, as Adam (ibid.:86) observes: 'The postwar hegemony of the United States, especially among the advanced capitalist nations, as well as among much of the third world, has also had an impact upon the social organization of homosexuality and the development of a political movement'. Consequently, my use of some Australian sources in the following discussion of gay liberation demonstrates not so much the specifically Australian character as the American inflection of the Australian gay liberation movement.

Nationally and internationally, gay liberation was neither a monolithic nor even an entirely coherent social movement. It was organised around analyses of the structures of lesbian and gay oppression, and how such oppression might be overcome. Homosexuality was represented as an identity repressed by heterosexist power structures which privilege gender-asymmetry, sexual reproduction and the patriarchal nuclear family. Unlike the homophile movement, gay liberation theorised that the system would never be radically transformed by those who were invested in it. Dominant formulations of sex and gender categories (and the institutions which supported them) would be eradicated only by gay men and lesbians who, refusing to accept their subaltern status, would destroy the system through literal and symbolic acts of violence. A gay identity was a revolutionary identity: what it sought was not social recognition but to overthrow the social institutions which marginalised and pathologised homosexuality. In so far as homosexuality did not conform to normative understandings of sex and gender, in liberationist discourse it was often represented as heralding the subversion of those categories, and enabling a new and unmediated sexuality for all people.

In adopting the rhetoric of revolution used by other new social movements, gay liberation assumed a much more aggressive and less conciliatory strategy than the homophile movement had advocated: 'Gay liberationists targeted the same institutions as homophile militants', D'Emilio (1983:234) observes, 'but their disaffection from American society impelled them to use tactics that their predecessors would never have adopted'. After all, a major catalyst of emergent gay activism in North America was dissatisfaction with the homophile movement's reluctance to challenge the dominant psychiatric evaluation of homosexuality as a sickness. Instead of trying (as homophile organisations had done) to persuade psychiatrists to adopt more liberal and less pathological understandings of homosexuality, gay liberationists spoke out against such 'expert' opinions, and insisted that their personal experiences be recognised as authoritative. American gay liberationists disrupted the annual conventions of both the American Medical Association and the American Psychiatric Association in order to protest against the continued pathologisation of homosexuality (Alinder, 1992:141–4; Chicago Gay Liberation Front, 1992:145–7). Like the anti-psychiatrist slogan, 'Off the couches, into the streets', the activist demand that psychiatrists 'refer their homosexual patients to gay liberation' is evidence of the liberationist belief that the psychological distress of homosexuals living in a homophobic culture could be relieved by political rather than psychiatric intervention (Chicago Gay Liberation Front, 1992: 146). Australian gay liberation newsletters frequently ran articles critiquing the psychiatric assessment of homosexuality (Jeff, 1972; Wills, 1972; Watson, 1974). They tend to advocate either the peer support of gay consciousness-raising groups as an alternative to psychiatric intervention, or the services of gay-affirmative psychiatrists.

What distinguished liberationist from homophile strategies was the public assumption of gay identity and the discrediting of professional opinion. These tactics were used in challenging not only psychiatric and medical models of homosexuality but also in many other gay interventions. The assertion of homosexuality as a politicised identity and insistence on the validity of gay-inflected knowledges are both enabled in the liberationist model by an emphasis on 'coming out' and consciousness-raising. Gay liberationists promoted the coming-out narrative—an unambiguous and public declaration of one's homosexuality—as a potent means of social transformation. An Australian gay newsletter from this period typifies the gay liberationist emphasis on the multi-directional effects of coming out. Subtitled 'Are You Proud To Be Gay?', it reads:

> We believe that it is so important to remind everyone you are a homosexual—COMING OUT—for yourself so you won't be subjected to anti-homosexual acts against yourself, and so other homosexuals who haven't come-out [sic] or are not confident of their homosexuality can realize other people are homosexuals and that they enjoy it. (*Gay Pride Week News*, 1973, 1)

Here the logics of coming out assume that homosexuality is not simply a private aspect of the individual, relevant only to friends and colleagues. Instead, it is potentially a transformative identity that must be avowed publicly until it is no longer a shameful secret but a legitimately recognised way of being in the world.

Consciousness-raising groups, more commonly associated with second-wave feminism, were also important in providing homosexuals with a forum for supportive discussion and personal growth. Eschewing hierarchical formations, they assumed peer relations between the members of the group, and valued experience more than expertise. Consciousness-raising assumed that gay men and women would have many experiences of oppression in common, and that uncensored discussions of these experiences would lead both to personal empowerment and a collective understanding of homophobic culture (A Gay Male Group, 1992:293–301). Typically, consciousness-raising groups discussed such matters as growing up, sexual experiences and relations with family members. It was assumed that the knowledge generated in these sessions, as well as the new modes of conduct established to facilitate fair and sincere discussion, would enable a range of transformations, such as the refashioning of gay relationships and community ethics to education and law reform.

There was much talk in gay liberationist circles about the necessity to create conditions in which people would be valued as people, rather than in terms of what was described in liberationist rhetoric as their 'sex roles'. Homosexual oppression was theorised overwhelmingly in terms of gender, since 'male homosexuals share the oppression of patriarchy in that our sexuality, if not our general behaviour, is believed to be non-masculine' (Hurley and Johnston, 1975:24). There was much discussion about rejecting the constraints of gender, most radically by the small effeminist movement which celebrated effeminacy in gay men on the grounds that it refused even those patriarchal privileges enjoyed by straight-acting gay men. Effeminists opposed sexism, and urged gay liberationists to be more attentive to the imperatives of feminism:

> Feminism destroys male myths of gender roles and the nuclear family (basic ideological units for the effective functioning of capitalist patriarchy). it [sic] destroys state and laissez-faire capitalism and the erotic procreative dichotomy which the system inflicts on us. If eroticism and reproduction are seen as possibly separate entities and that [sic] masculine and feminine roles are negated as limiting factors in human development the homosexual person is automatically liberated. (Hawkins, 1975:23)

Gay liberation frequently understood itself to be challenging that system which, in representing certain gender roles as natural, stabilised heterosexual privilege. 'To protect the power of straight men in a sexist society', writes Allen Young (1992:29) 'homosexuality becomes prohibited behavior. As gays, we demand an end to the gender programming which starts when we are born'.

Gay liberation philosophy aimed to secure more than tolerance for homosexuality. It was committed to a radical and extensive transformation of social structures and values. In understanding that gender and sex roles oppress everyone, gay liberation sought not only recognition of homosexuality as a legitimate identity for a minority population but also to 'free the homosexual in everyone' (Wittman, 1992: 341). Or as Martha Shelley (1992:34) puts it:

promote homosexuality behavior or recognize that it is instilled in all of us?

I will tell you what we want, we radical homosexuals: not for you to tolerate us, or to accept us, but to understand us. And this you can only do by becoming one of us. We want to reach the homosexuals entombed in you, to liberate our brothers and sisters, locked in the prisons of your skulls.

Gay liberation did not imagine a future in which everyone would be homosexual. What it claimed is that homosexuality has the potential to liberate forms of sexuality unstructured by the constraints of sex and gender.

Although gay liberation was organised primarily around gay identity and gay pride, initially it had political affinities with other sexually marginal identities like bisexuals, drag queens, transvestites and transsexuals. The principles of gay liberation benefited a range of other identificatory categories. Drag queens and transvestites were prominent in the Stonewall riots (D'Emilio, 1983:231–3) and sometimes featured with other sexual minorities in early gay liberationist rhetoric. In discussing the development of American gay liberation, Altman (1972:113–16) observes that while gay liberationists were most commonly male, 'white, middle-class, [and] educated'—the gay identity subsequently consolidated during the civil rights phase of the gay movement—a small number of transvestites, transsexuals and hermaphrodites were evident at the fringes of the movement. This liberationist expansiveness is clearly articulated in a gay manifesto published in 1974 in a special issue of an Australian university newspaper. Its list of basic demands includes 'full recognition of the individual's right to change sex and the right to all necessary medical treatment free' (Anon., 1974:5).

Gay liberationists supported other sexual minorities not just because heterosexual society regarded them as gay or even because of a certain undeniable overlapping of subcultures. Rather, gay liberation understood that the marginalisation and devaluation of homosexuality was effected by that dominant and rigidly hierarchical conceptualisation of sex and gender which constituted the social norm. In order to liberate homosexuality, gay liberation was committed to eradicating fixed notions of femininity and masculinity: that move would similarly liberate any other group oppressed by what it critiqued as normative sex and gender roles. Liberationist rhetoric usually saw gay liberation as possible only in the context of what Altman (1972:58) calls 'a much broader sexual liberation' brought about by transformation of social attitudes to gender and sexuality. It was understood in early gay liberationist rhetoric that if those social transformations identified as essential to the liberation of homosexuals were achieved, then inevitably they would also liberate sexuality itself.

In a chapter entitled 'Liberation: Toward the Polymorphous Whole', Dennis Altman identifies various goals of liberation. These include eradicating sex roles, transforming the family as an institution; ending homophobic violence; the demise of monolithic categories of homosexuality and heterosexuality in favour of a potential bisexuality; developing a new vocabulary of the erotic; and understanding sexuality as pleasurable and relational, rather than reproductive or as an index of status. He defines liberation as 'freedom from the surplus repression that prevents us from recognizing our essential androgynous and erotic natures', and 'freedom for the fulfillment [sic] of human potential' (Altman, 1972:83). Gay liberationists believed that traditional conceptualisations of sex and gender constrained people from recognising, in essentialist terms, their true selves. A world in which sex was of no consequence and gender ceased to exist would enable the development of that bisexual potentiality which, gay liberationists argued, was repressed by the imperative to recognise oneself as either heterosexual or homosexual:

how did this imperative dominate... where was this need developed — needs deconstruction

The non-repressed person recognizes his bisexual potential; he is not some ideal person midway along the Kinsey behavioral scale. People would still fall in love and form relationships, and those relationships would be homosexual as well as

and laws transpired out of religious doctrine

heterosexual. What would be different is that the social difference between the two would vanish, and once this happened, we would lose the feeling of being limited, of having to choose between an exclusively straight or exclusively gay world. (ibid.:94) *other than religious morality ...what are other ways as to why this hasn't happened... science?*

Once gender is theorised as an oppressive system of classification, both heterosexuality and homosexuality come to be understood as merely 'artificial categories' (Young, 1992:29). Since heterosexuality and homosexuality are defined in terms of gender relations, gay liberation posited that those categories were assumed only for strategic purposes and would be abandoned once gender distinctions were no longer meaningful. As Judy Grahn argues, 'if anyone were allowed to fall in love with *anyone*, the word "homosexual" would not be needed' (quoted in Third World Gay Revolution, 1992:258). Such assertions were common: 'Gay revolution will produce a world in which all social and sensual relationships will be gay and in which homo- and heterosexuality will be incomprehensible terms' (Gay Revolution Party Manifesto, 1992:344). While gay liberation was committed to radically altering the ways in which homosexuality was conceptualised, it understood that the achievement of its goals would put an end to the very categories of homosexuality and heterosexuality by which it currently understood itself. But as Altman (1972:227) observes, 'if man/ womankind reaches the point where it is able to dispense with the categories of homo- and heterosexuality, the loss will be well worth the gain'.

Gay liberation transformed homophile reform into an international mass movement. Enabled in part by the often unacknowledged work of the homophile movement, the achievements of the gay liberation movement are considerable. Never quite the revolutionary force it represented itself as being, gay liberation altered western social organisation irrevocably by generating a public (and not simply sexual) gay identity that functioned in politically effective ways. Although it did not succeed in creating that genderless society in which terms like 'heterosexuality' and 'homosexuality' would be merely descriptive, gay liberation articulated a substantial and influential critique of gender as an

42

oppressive construction propping up heterosexuality. Although that denaturalisation of gender is perhaps the most compelling connection between liberationist and later queer theories, there are many other connections between gay liberation and queer. Assessing the contemporary relevance of republishing, twenty years later, the 1972 gay liberation classic edited by Karla Jay and Allen Young, *Out of the Closets*, Michael Warner (1992:18) notes that 'its republication shows that many insights and aspirations now associated with queer theory have long histories—including self-conscious dialogue among lesbians as well as between lesbians and gay men, about their multiple differences' (cf. Chinn and Franklin, 1993). Many of the ideological assumptions of gay liberation are very much in evidence in the 1990s. Yet its promotion of identity, its commitment to some 'natural' and polymorphous sexuality underlying social organisation, its understanding of power predominantly in terms of repression and its belief in the possibility of large-scale social transformation or liberation are all challenged by the new knowledges and practices mobilised around queer.

Lesbian Feminism

Although small numbers of women had always been involved in gay liberation, and equally small numbers of lesbians in the women's movement, lesbians increasingly felt that they were marginalised in both. There are precedents for such dissatisfaction. As early as 1904 Anna Rühling addressed members of Hirschfeld's Scientific Humanitarian Committee on the relations between the women's and the homosexual movements. She drew attention to the fact that the women's movement refused to deal with the issue of homosexuality:

> When we consider all the gains that homosexual women have for decades achieved for the women's movement it can only be regarded as astounding that the big and influential organizations of this movement have up to now not raised one finger to secure for their not insignificant number of Uranian members their just rights as far as the state and society are concerned. (quoted in Lauritsen and Thorstad, 1974:18–19)

The mainstream homophile movement's indifference to issues of gender similarly prompted the Daughters of Bilitis to recognise the need to address lesbians specifically instead of subsuming them in the purportedly generic category of homosexuality. Gay men and lesbians have their homosexuality—that is, their same-sex object choice—in common. But the gendering of that sexuality has produced substantial cultural differences between them. 'Lesbians and gays are not two genders within one sexual category', writes Jeffrey Weeks (1985:203). 'They have different histories, which are differentiated because of the complex organisation of male and female identities, precisely along lines of gender.' Historically speaking, for example, the masculine relation to sexuality has been figured differently from the feminine. Access to employment and an independent income has been both easier and more profitable for men than for women and, in criminal law, homosexuality has been constituted almost exclusively as a masculine proclivity.

As the gay and women's movements developed in the late 1960s and early 1970s, some lesbians who had never identified as feminist continued to work with gay men, and others aligned themselves with both movements. But a significant number began to analyse specifically the political position of lesbians. Often a difficult project, it encountered some indifference and even resistance from official gay liberationist or feminist organisations. In spite of repeated interventions by lesbians, gay liberation tended to ignore as marginal models that would accommodate feminist demands. As Laurie Bebbington and Margaret Lyons (1975:27) pointed out to male gay liberationists: 'the discussion of homosexuality and feminism is the opportunity . . . to confront your role as men in a patriarchal society and to recognize the ways in which your sexism oppresses us, as lesbians'. Initially the feminist movement was careful to distance itself officially from lesbianism, feeling that such an association would damage what was seen as the more fundamental project of securing equal rights for women. Betty Friedan, a pioneering second-wave feminist and author of the influential book, *The Feminine Mystique* (1965), saw militant lesbianism as potentially undermining feminist gains and has been credited with naming the nascent lesbian movement 'a lavender menace'. Setting her right on this matter, Susan Brownmiller nevertheless describes militant lesbians as 'a lavender herring perhaps, but surely no clear and present danger' (quoted in Echols, 1989:345). The feminist refusal to advocate lesbian rights was not always, however, merely a strategic gesture. Ti-Grace Atkinson, a prominent American feminist, dismissed lesbianism as foundationally antithetical to the feminist agenda, because it 'involves role-playing and, more important, because it is based on the primary assumption of male oppression' and thus 'reinforces the sex class system' (quoted in ibid.: 211).[1]

Despite this inauspicious start, lesbians continued to organise—at first covertly, and then directly—their challenge to the institutionalised homophobia and sexism of the women's and gay liberation movements. In the 1990s, when feminism is routinely understood to include a commitment to opposing homophobia, it might seem logical that the women's movement would consider lesbian demands for recognition and equality as quintessentially feminist. However, in their at times autobiographical account of the history of the women's and lesbian movements, Sidney Abbott and Barbara Love (1973:108) note that 'when Women's Liberation got under way in the mid-1960's, attitudes about Lesbians were virtually the same inside and outside the movement'. The institutional struggle for recognition by lesbians in the United States women's movement was first focused on the organisational structures of the largest and most influential women's liberation group, the National Organisation for Women (NOW). As in the case of other women's liberation groups, lesbians were involved at every level in the NOW hierarchy but their lesbianism was either unknown to the organisation or was scrupulously managed as potential damage. Originally—and to this day—a conservative feminist organisation, NOW describes itself in terms of equal rights rather than women's liberation. It has sought liberal rather than radical solutions to what it saw as the problem of women's inequality.

The issue of lesbianism slowly became an irresolvable problem for NOW as calls for its recognition were blocked by influential figures in the organisation. Dissatisfied with NOW, a number of women resigned and called a meeting to discuss discrimination against lesbians—what was then described as 'sexism'—in the women's movement.[2] That event 'was historic in that it was the first meeting of radical young Lesbians without gay men, the first time Gay Liberation Front women had met with Lesbians from the women's movement, and the first time Lesbians from the women's movement had met each other as Lesbians' (Abbott and Love, 1973:113). There it was decided that a collectively written position paper, outlining the political connections between lesbianism and feminism, should be circulated among heterosexual feminist groups and launched at the Second Congress to Unite Women.

Accordingly, when the Second Congress opened in May 1970, it was disrupted by twenty women who, resignifying the slur of Friedan's nomination, called themselves 'Lavender Menace'. The lights went out, and when they 'came up again, twenty women wearing T-shirts imprinted "Lavender Menace" stood at the front of the room' (Schneir, 1994:160). For two hours these activists spoke to the four hundred feminists about their experience and analysis of discrimination against lesbians in the women's movement. The next day members of Lavender Menace conducted workshops on lesbianism and homophobia; at the final assembly of the Congress, four statements put forward by the group were adopted as resolutions:

> Be it resolved that Women's Liberation is a lesbian plot.
>
> Resolved that whenever the label lesbian is used against the movement collectively or against women individually, it is to be affirmed, not denied.
>
> In all discussions of birth control, homosexuality must be included as a legitimate method of contraception.   *word*
>
> All sex education curricula must include lesbianism as a valid, legitimate form of sexual expression and love. (quoted in Marotta, 1981:244–5)

Also circulated at the Congress was a paper on 'The Woman-Identified Woman', written by Lavender Menace who subsequently renamed themselves Radicalesbians. This influential paper first appeared in the counter-cultural publications *Rat* and *Come Out!* before being printed as a pamphlet by Gay Flames and then reprinted in numerous anthologies. In many ways, it exemplifies the political position of lesbian feminism. As its title makes clear, it deflects attention from lesbianism as a sexual orientation or practice in order to reconceptualise it as a way of being in the world that, potentially, includes all women. The perspective gained from lesbian experience—'the liberation of self, the inner peace, the real love of self and of all women'—is in the words of the Radicalesbians (quoted in Schneir, 1994:162) 'something to be shared with all women—because we are all women'.

In 'The Woman-Identified Woman' lesbianism is inscribed as *redefining the word lesbian* a political stance rather than a sexual identification: '[a] lesbian is the rage of all women condensed to the point of explosion' (ibid.). The Radicalesbians' paper aligns lesbians much more closely with heterosexual women than with male homosexuals, arguing that the hatred directed against lesbians is an effect of male domination:

> *very diff from Male gay Liberation* Lesbian is the word, the label, the condition that holds women in line . . . Lesbian is a label invented by the Man to throw at any woman who dares to be his equal, who dares to challenge his prerogatives (including that of all women as part of the exchange medium among men), who dares to assert the primacy of her own needs. (ibid.:163)

As a corollary, 'The Woman-Identified Woman' argues that lesbianism is the logical extension of feminism: 'it is the primacy of women relating to women, of women creating a new consciousness of and with each other which is at the heart of women's liberation, and the basis for the cultural revolution' (ibid.:167). Although NOW remained divided for a further turbulent year on the issue of lesbianism, towards the end of 1971 it passed a series of resolutions which incorporated many of the sentiments expressed in 'The Woman-Identified Woman' paper:

> Be it resolved that NOW recognizes the double oppression of lesbians;

> Be it resolved that a woman's right to her own person includes the right to define and express her own sexuality and choose her own life-style and

> Be it resolved that NOW acknowledges the oppression of lesbians as a legitimate concern of feminism. (quoted in Abbott and Love, 1973:134)

'The Woman-Identified Woman' paper was both the cause and the effect of lesbian feminist mobilisation in the 1970s. In an account such as this, however, which maps the changing categories of sexual identification, it is equally important for another reason. In spite of its now dated hipness—its references to 'sisters' and 'the Man'—and its recourse to a version of popular psychology that promotes wholeness and self-love, many of its conceptualisations continue to influence those writings that constitute the theoretical grounds of lesbian feminism. Much of this lesbian feminist writing is informed by the twin demands of collective activism and intellectual theorising, and it is characterised by an amalgam of political analysis and strategies for cultural transformation.

The lesbian feminist position as it developed in the 1980s is outlined in Adrienne Rich's enormously influential and often cited essay, 'Compulsory Heterosexuality and Lesbian Existence'. Rich's essay—written in 1978 and first published in *Signs* in 1980—was controversial and generated much theoretical discussion (see Ann Ferguson et al., 1981). Subsequently, Rich claimed that one motive for writing it had been 'to sketch, at least, some bridge over the gap between *lesbian* and *feminist*' (Rich, 1986:24). Given that goal it is not surprising that Rich's essay, like 'The Woman-Identified Woman', should foreground the position of lesbians as women: 'If we consider the possibility that all women . . . exist on a lesbian continuum, we can see ourselves as moving in and out of this continuum, whether we identify ourselves as lesbian or not' (ibid.: 54). Moreover, Rich's representation of lesbianism as something understood most productively within categories of gender actively distanced her version of lesbianism from any equivalent affiliation with gay men:

> Lesbians have historically been deprived of a political existence through 'inclusion' as female versions of male homosexuality. To equate lesbian existence with male homosexuality because each is stigmatised is to erase female reality once again. Part of the history of lesbian existence is, obviously, to be found where lesbians, lacking a coherent female community, have shared a kind of social life and common cause with homosexual men. But there are differences: women's lack of economic and cultural privilege relative to men; qualitative differences in female and male relationships—for example, the patterns of

anonymous sex among male homosexuals, and the pro-
nounced ageism in male homosexual standards of sexual attractiveness. I perceive the lesbian experience as being, like
motherhood, a profoundly *female* experience, with particular
oppressions, meanings, and potentialities we cannot comprehend as long as we simply bracket it with other sexually stigmatized existences. (ibid.:318–19)

This passage signals an important shift in the theorising of lesbianism and one which continues to inform debates about the
political efficacy of queer. Although not calling simply for a
gender-specific description of lesbianism, it argues that for lesbians, gender, not sexuality, is the primary identificatory category.
Rich does not simply value gender over sexuality. She understands
it as the exemplary paradigm for oppression of every sort: 'the
power men everywhere wield over women . . . has become a
model for every other form of exploitation and illegal control'
(ibid.:68). Consequently women (rather than gay men) are the
natural political allies of lesbians. Gay men, in so far as they are
men, are part of an oppressive social structure which lesbian
feminism is committed to overthrowing.

Rich modifies this argument significantly in a footnote added
to her essay in 1986: 'I now think we have much to learn both
from the uniquely female aspects of lesbian existence and from
the complex "gay" identity we share with gay men' (ibid.:53).
Although Rich here alters the original emphasis of her essay, a significant strand of lesbian feminism has continued to identify gay
men as complicit in the structures of male domination, and consequently as less suitable allies of lesbians than heterosexual women. Sheila Jeffreys, for instance, emphasises a solidarity between
women and lesbians—a solidarity assumed to be axiomatic to
feminism itself—while disallowing any comparable alliance
between lesbians and gay men. By valuing identity categories
underwritten by gender more highly than those underwritten by
sexuality, Jeffreys foregrounds 'the whole system of male
supremacy' in order to make the broad and gender-inflected argument that all men—gay men included—oppress women (Jeffreys,
1994:460). Moreover, she singles out gay men as having a pecu-

liarly potent function in this general oppression: 'Gay men have an influential role in defining what the feminine is in male supremacist culture through their involvement in the media and fashion industries' (ibid.:461). The representation of gay men as the epitome of patriarchal values has a regrettably homophobic history in feminist theory. For example, in addition to the essay by Rich discussed already, it recurs in the writings of Irigaray (1981:107–11) and Frye (1983) and is critiqued by Fuss (1989:45–9). Significantly, gay liberationist thought offers an opposing analysis of how gay men relate to the oppression of women: it argues that gay men can work against 'male chauvinism' more easily than heterosexual men because they are not so fully invested in the system (cf. Wittman, 1992:332).

While there is obviously something to be said for considering the ways in which gender operates in the field of power, Jeffreys's reductive focus on gender overlooks other and equally significant variables. Approvingly paraphrasing one of Marilyn Frye's arguments, Jeffreys (1994:468) observes that 'gay men can be seen as the conformists to male supremacy because they choose to love those whom everyone is mandated to love under this political system, that is, men. Lesbians, on the other hand, choose to love those who are despised, that is, women'. If gay men, as Jeffreys suggests, conform to male supremacy via the gender of their sexual object choices, it follows that the non-conformists to male supremacy are those who love women, namely, lesbians and *heterosexual men*. Here, Jeffreys's relentless focus on gender produces a conclusion that works against the terms of her own argument. Inadvertently, she demonstrates Sedgwick's point (1990:32) that 'it is unrealistic to expect a close, textured analysis of same-sex relations through an optic calibrated in the first place to the coarser stigmata of gender difference'.

Even the title of Marilyn Frye's chapter on 'Lesbian Feminism and the Gay Rights Movement: Another View of Male Supremacy, Another Separatism' economically suggests both an affinity between lesbians and heterosexual women and an antipathy between gay men and lesbians. Frye (1983:129) observes a tendency to assume 'a cultural and political affinity between gay men on the one hand and women—lesbians and/or feminists—on the other' because each group is differently but equivalently marginalised in dominant understandings of the sex/gender system. Frye counters this popular assumption by arguing that

> a look at some of the principles and values of male-supremacist society and culture suggests immediately that the male gay rights movement and gay male culture, as they can be known in their public manifestations, are in many central points considerably more congruent than discrepant with this phallocracy, which in turn is so hostile to women and to the woman-loving to which lesbians are committed. (ibid.:130)

Those 'principles and values' which, according to Frye, connect heterosexual and homosexual men in bonds of indissoluble masculinity include a commitment to the rights of the male citizen, homo-eroticism, hatred of women, and compulsory male heterosexuality. Taking a harder line than either Rich or Jeffreys, Frye considers these alleged affinities between phallocratic culture and the gay liberation movement. But she does so only to conclude that, far from being just like heterosexual men, 'gay men generally are in significant ways, perhaps in all important ways, only more loyal to masculinity and male-supremacy than other men' (ibid.:132).

Frye is neither the first nor the last lesbian feminist theorist to argue that the male bonding that enables heterosexual exchanges differs in degree rather than kind from the male bonding that sustains homosexuality. However, her counter-intuitive claim that gay and heterosexual men are equally committed to 'compulsory male heterosexuality' is worth considering in some detail, because it is more idiosyncratic and may well be the most extreme form of her argument. Having established—more to her own satisfaction than mine—that heterosexual and gay cultures are unified in their love of men and their hatred of women, Frye (ibid.:140) goes on to outline the rationale behind compulsory male heterosexuality: 'It is very important to the maintenance of male-supremacy that men fuck women, a lot. So it is required; it is compulsory. Doing it is both doing one's duty and an expression of solidarity'.

The discourse of gay liberation might appear opposed, or at least disloyal, to this requirement. However, while acknowledging that gay men are generally not interested in 'doing [their] duty' in this sense, Frye argues that it is only because they have an over-developed hatred for women:

> In many cases [gay men] are loath to do their duty only because they have learned all too well their lessons in women-hating. Their reluctance to play out this part of manhood is due only to an imbalance, where the requisite woman-hating has taken a form and intensity which puts it in tension with this other requirement of manhood. (ibid.)

There are obvious problems with this analysis, which treats both a desire for and an aversion to having sex with women as evidence of the same basic contempt for them. Furthermore, that 'solidarity' which Frye discerns between gay and heterosexual men goes largely unacknowledged by both groups. Frye partially notes this problem—for which she offers no solution—when she observes in passing that 'it becomes something of a puzzle why straight men do not recognize their gay brothers' (ibid.:130). Her insistence on the primacy of gender in structuring oppression represents the projects of lesbian feminism and gay liberation as mutually incommensurable: 'Far from there being a natural affinity between feminist lesbians and the gay civil rights movement, I see their politics as being, in most respects, directly antithetical to each other' (ibid.:145). This assumption has generated a great deal of debate. Although it is far from being a requisite characteristic of lesbian feminism, it continues to inform representational struggles over sexual identification.

'Compulsory heterosexuality' is also, of course, a key idea for Rich, who coined the phrase. Unlike Frye, however, she considers the effect of this regulatory order principally as it pertains to women, identifying heterosexuality as 'a *political institution*' which systematically works to the disadvantage of all women (Rich, 1986:313). In this respect, she expands the argument (taken up previously in 'The Woman-Identified Woman') that 'as long as male acceptability is primary—both to individual women and to the movement as a whole—the term "lesbian" will be used effectively against women' (Schneir, 1994:165). For Rich, heterosexuality is not simply a matter of personal choice in the volitional

sense implied by a phrase like 'sexual preference'. In comparing
heterosexuality to capitalism and racism, she represents it as structured across a fundamental imbalance of power: 'The failure to
examine heterosexuality as an institution is like failing to admit
that the economic system called capitalism or the caste system of
racism is maintained by a variety of forces, including both physical violence and false consciousness' (Rich, 1986:51). She draws
attention to the ways in which both the naturalisation of heterosexuality and the pathologisation of lesbianism work to privilege
heterosexual masculinity.

Having identified 'the lie of compulsory female heterosexuality',
Rich goes on to anticipate its undoing (ibid.:61). When underwritten by feminist analysis and commitment, lesbianism—'a form
of naysaying to patriarchy, an act of resistance' (ibid.:52)—
denaturalises heterosexuality by demonstrating its ideological
investments:

> we can say there is a *nascent* feminist political content in the
> act of choosing a woman lover or life partner in the face of
> institutionalized heterosexuality. But for lesbian existence to
> realize this political content in an ultimately liberating form, the
> erotic choice must deepen and expand into conscious woman
> identification—into lesbian feminism. (ibid.:66)

Although careful to point out that lesbianism is not necessarily
radical in itself, Rich represents it as offering feminism a model for
radical transformation, a model that identifies and resolves that
contradiction at the heart of feminism as it was then primarily
constituted.

Rich's essay denaturalises heterosexuality by naturalising the
categories of gender. Monique Wittig's essays, on the other hand,
are just as committed to challenging heterosexual hegemony, but
destabilise the presumption of gender that underwrites Rich's
analysis. In this respect, Wittig's work extends the sketchy account
offered by Radicalesbians of the relation between gender—or, as
they put it, 'sex roles'—and sexuality:

> Lesbianism, like male homosexuality, is a category of behaviour
> possible only in a sexist society characterized by rigid sex roles
> and dominated by male supremacy . . . Homosexuality is a by-

product of a particular way of setting up roles (or approved patterns of behavior) on the basis of sex; as such it is an inauthentic (not consonant with 'reality') category. In a society in which men do not oppress women, and sexual expression is allowed to follow feelings, the categories of homosexuality and heterosexuality would disappear. (Schneir, 1994:162–3)

'The Woman-Identified Woman' essay assumes that gender underpins heterosexuality and homosexuality equally, and implies that the destruction of sex roles will be followed by polymorphous perversity in the form of utopian bisexuality. This position is akin ✹ to that of early gay liberation. Rich is fairly dismissive of the futuristic imaginings of gay liberationists and lesbian feminists. Confronted with 'the frequently heard assertion that in a world of genuine equality, where men are nonoppressive and nurturing, everyone would be bisexual', she critiques it on the grounds that 'it is a liberal leap across the tasks and struggles of here and now, the continuing process of sexual definition which will generate its own possibilities and choices' (Rich, 1986:34, 35).

According to Wittig, however, the categories of gender are entirely complicit in the maintenance of heterosexuality. This is why she places lesbianism outside the field of gender altogether. In accepting the categories of gender—even if only to critique them—'we naturalize the social phenomena which express our oppression, making change impossible' (Wittig, 1992:11). To perceive that gender is not the cause but the effect of oppression is to understand that '"woman" has meaning only in heterosexual systems of thought and heterosexual economic systems' (ibid.:32). Wittig thus represents lesbianism as triumphantly in excess of gender categories:

> To destroy 'woman' does not mean that we aim . . . to destroy lesbianism simultaneously with the categories of sex . . . Lesbian is the only concept I know of which is beyond the categories of sex (woman and man), because the designated subject (lesbian) is *not* a woman, either economically, or politically, or ideologically. (ibid.:20)

Here only lesbians enjoy this transcendental position. Yet in an earlier essay, Wittig implies that gay men are positioned similarly

replacing woman w/ lesbian. woman does n't exist

in relation to the categories of gender: 'If we, as lesbians and gay men, continue to speak of ourselves and conceive of ourselves as women and as men, we are instrumental in maintaining heterosexuality' (ibid.:30). Although her terms resemble those used by Radicalesbians, Rich and Frye, Wittig develops a significantly different argument. Her reification of 'lesbian' has been critiqued by later theorists, who find her utopian celebration of the category unpersuasive even within the terms of her own argument (cf. Butler, 1990:120–2; Fuss, 1989:43). Nevertheless, recent theorising of sexual identities has taken up her emphasis on the constitutive power of discourse, her insistence that the category 'woman'—like the category 'man'—is not a foundational truth but 'only an imaginary formation' (Wittig, 1992:15), and her representation of lesbians and gay men as similarly positioned subjects.

Often represented as a coherent movement, both puritanical and prescriptive, lesbian feminism actually describes a range of sometimes contradictory political and theoretical positions. Even a brief summary of lesbian feminist theory demonstrates that its rearticulations of sexuality through gender do not necessarily produce identical or even compatible analyses. Although it is common to represent lesbian feminism and queer as oppositional political impulses (Jeffreys, 1993; Wolfe and Penelope, 1993), some of queer's most trenchant demonstrations of how gender functions in licensing heterosexuality as normative originate in early lesbian feminist theorising. This point is made by Rosemary Hennessy (1994:93) when objecting to the way in which connections between 1970s lesbian feminism and 1990s queer theory have been largely disavowed:

Almost twenty years ago, lesbian feminists in the West—among them, Charlotte Bunch, The Furies, The Purple September Staff and Monique Wittig—called for a critique of heterosexuality. They argued that feminism, including discussions of lesbianism among cultural feminists, dealt with sexuality as a personal or civil rights issue in order to avoid a broader ranging materialist critique of the normative status of heterosexuality . . . It seems to me that these knowledges offer a rich and radical tradition for developing postmodern materialist queer theory.

With its coalitional politics and its emphasis on sexual identifications, queer's affinity is clearly with that strand of lesbian feminism that does not understand sexuality as the by-product of gender. Queer is also productively informed by lesbian feminism in three crucial respects: its attention to the specificity of gender, its framing of sexuality as institutional rather than personal, and its critique of compulsory heterosexuality.

6

Limits of Identity

The homophile movement began by outlining principles more radical than those it eventually came to represent. Similarly, both the lesbian and gay liberation movements evolved into social movements so culturally concretised and elaborate that the tenets and values they represented came to be seen as hegemonic, and were resisted in turn by further marginalised groups. Initially gay liberation and lesbian feminism advocated a wholesale sexual revolution; increasingly they consolidated themselves as civil rights movements intent on securing equality for marginalised minority groups. As Altman (1982:211) notes:

> One of the ways in which the gay liberation movement of a decade ago differed from most of its predecessors was in its insistence that only radical change to society could bring about genuine acceptance of homosexuality. The thrust of the gay movement over the past decade has been away from this perception toward the idea that all that is involved is the granting of civil rights to a new minority.

Where once both lesbian and gay activists had focused on the radical reformulation of the sex/gender system, increasingly they concentrated on securing equality for a homosexual population defined in terms of same-sex object choice. 'By the mid-1970s', writes D'Emilio (1992a:xxvi), 'phrases like "sexual orientation" and the "gay minority" had entered the lexicon of the movement'. In retrospective accounts of these movements, it is common to read that gay liberation and lesbian feminism lost their radical edge in a conservative slide from oppositional to assimilationist politics. It is certainly helpful to think about why the strategies of these two movements changed and how their positions shifted with regard to dominant cultural institutions. Yet such things cannot be explained simply in terms of a narrative of deterioration. Instead of assuming that gay liberation and lesbian feminism finally yielded to the pressures and rewards of social conformity, it is possible to think of these movements as operating within changing conceptions of social transformation.

Steven Seidman argues along these lines when mapping the historical shift of these new social movements from the liberationist to the ethnic model of gay identity. Seidman (1993:110) argues that initially the gay and lesbian feminist movements represented themselves in terms of liberation: 'Liberation theory presupposed a notion of an innate polymorphous, androgynous human nature. Liberation politics aimed at freeing individuals from the constraints of a sex/gender system that locked them into mutually exclusive homo/hetero and feminine/masculine roles'. However, by the mid 1970s this liberationist framework became less important for both gay and lesbian movements who increasingly favoured an ethnic model which emphasised community identity and cultural difference:

> From a broadly conceived sexual and gender liberation movement, the dominant agenda of the male-dominated gay culture became community building and winning civil rights. The rise of an ethnic model of identity and politics in the gay male community found a parallel in the lesbian feminist culture, with its emphasis on unique female values and building a womans-culture (ibid.:117).

Gay liberation advocated a radical transformation of social values, arguing that gay liberation would be secured only after sex and gender categories had been eradicated. Although subscribing to a different values-system and a different agenda for social transformation, the classic articulation of lesbian feminism is equally liberationist in arguing for specifically female subjects:

Any woman could be a lesbian. It was a revolutionary political choice which, if adopted by millions of women, would lead to the destabilisation of male supremacy as men lost the foundation of their power in women's selfless and unpaid, domestic, sexual, reproductive, economic and emotional servicing . . . It was to be an alternative universe in which we could construct a new sexuality, a new ethics, a new culture in opposition to malestream culture. (Jeffreys, 1993:ix)

Despite their differences, both the gay and the lesbian feminist models of liberation are intent on transforming oppressive social structures by representing same-sex sexual practices as legitimate. In emphasising the malleability of gender and sexuality, each has an avowedly constructionist understanding of sexuality. It is worth making this point because too often the positions taken up by gay liberation and lesbian feminism are dismissed as crudely essentialist. Douglas Crimp (1993:314) disputes that view: 'We were gay, and upon our gayness, we built a political movement. But is this really what happened? Wasn't it an emerging political movement that enabled the enunciation of a gay—rather than homosexual or homophile—identity?'

The shift in emphasis from a liberationist to an ethnic model of identity is explicable partly in terms of a general disillusionment with the grand scale of the liberationist project, sustained by 'a millenial notion of a liberated humanity free from constraining normative structures', and partly as a result of a gradual revaluation of the ways in which strategies of power and hence resistance are deployed (Seidman, 1993:116). Lesbians and gay men turned their attention increasingly to local sites of struggle and concentrated on securing specific rather than universal transformations of social structures. This shift in strategies or priorities has often been critiqued as a scaling-down of political intensity, as capitulation rather than as resistance to the hegemonic systems of the dominant social order. Consequently, Urvashi Vaid (1995) identifies the contradictory impulses of liberation and legitimation as blocking the contemporary lesbian and gay movement. 'Where's the Revolution?', asks Barbara Smith when recalling the liberationist logic of the mid 1970s in order to argue that subsequent versions of lesbian and gay politics are not only less ambitious but even wrong-headed versions of a once radical social critique:

> It was simply not possible for any oppressed people, including lesbians and gay men, to achieve freedom under this system . . . Nobody sane would want any part of the established order. It was the system—white supremacist, misogynistic, capitalistic and homophobic—that had made our lives so hard to begin with. We wanted something entirely new. Our movement was called lesbian and gay *liberation*, and more than a few of us, especially women and people of color, were working for a *revolution*. (Smith, 1993:13)

According to the liberationist model, the established social order is fundamentally corrupt, and therefore the success of any political action is to be measured by the extent to which it smashes that system. The ethnic model, by contrast, was committed to establishing gay identity as a legitimate minority group, whose official recognition would secure citizenship rights for lesbian and gay subjects.

Constructed as analogous to an ethnic minority—that is, as a distinct and identifiable population, rather than a radical potentiality for all—lesbians and gays can demand recognition and equal rights within the existing social system. Using the 'equal but different' logic of the civil rights movement, the ethnic model was conceived of as a strategic way of securing equal or increased legal protection for gay and lesbian subjects, establishing visible and commodified lesbian and gay urban communities, and legitimating 'gay' and 'lesbian' as categories of identification. 'By the end of the 1970s', writes Seidman (1994:172), 'the gay and lesbian movement had achieved such a level of subcultural elaboration and general social tolerance that a politics of cultural and social mainstreaming far overshadowed both the defensive strategies . . . and the revolutionary politics of the previous decades'. In its own terms, the ethnic model was successful, as is evident in the extent to which gay and lesbian identities are still organised significantly under its rubric. Yet the very characteristics that made possible its achievements also generated a substantial and irrecuperable dissatisfaction with the assumptions that underpinned its construction of a unified gay and lesbian identity.

The process of stabilisation—even solidification—enabled lesbians and gays to be represented as a coherent community, united by a collective lesbian and gay identity. That very process, however, disenfranchised subjects who might reasonably have expected to take up a position within any lesbian and gay constituency, or who felt better represented by the previous liberationist model. 'If early lesbian feminism emphasized the fluidity of identity categories and the importance of self-description', writes Arlene Stein (1991:44), 'with time the definition narrowed: Lesbians were biological women who do not sleep with men and who embrace the lesbian label'.[1]

At that historical moment when the dominant ethnic model constituted lesbian and gay subjects as a mainstream—albeit minority—group, processes of centralisation and marginalisation were repeated, and newly disaffected groups opposed or critiqued the notion of a singular or unified gay identity. Those alienated from the ethnic model consolidated by lesbian and gay identity did not simply demand to be included but also critiqued the fundamental principles which had centralised that specific (although supposedly universal) identity in the first place. Recalling the 'lavender menace' controversy, Gayle Rubin (1981) titles her pro-sado-masochism essay 'The Leather Menace', implying that lesbian feminists are just as culpable as second-wave feminists in maintaining normative identity categories. Since the success of the ethnic model of gay identity is to be gauged largely by the extent to which it has legitimised gay and lesbian identity in the dominant culture, it has difficulty in absorbing or controlling challenges to its authority from groups which are even more marginalised. In a specifically lesbian context, Stein (1991:45) argues that the problem 'was not so much that boundary-making took place—for it does in all identity-based movements—but that the discourse of the movement, rooted in notions of authenticity and inclusion, ran so completely counter to it'.

Ironically, given its origins in a race-based politics, the ethnic model's gay and lesbian subject was white. It was not simply that the lesbian and gay community described by the ethnic model happened to be predominantly white. Rather, in describing that community as organised by a single defining feature—sexual orientation—the ethnic model could theorise race only as an insubstantial or, at best, additional category of identification. Lesbians and gays of colour, frustrated by the assumption that they would have more in common with white lesbians and gay men than with their own ethnic or racial communities, began to critique both overt and covert racism in the mainstream gay community (cf. Jagose, 1994:14–16). Anthologies published in the 1980s— such as *This Bridge Called My Back: Writings By Radical Women of Color* (Moraga and Anzaldúa, 1983), *Twice Blessed: On Being Lesbian, Gay and Jewish* (Balka and Rose, 1989) and *In the Life* (Beam, 1986)—focused significantly on the meshings of racial and sexual identities. In different ways, these and similar essays critique the notion of a unitary lesbian and gay subject. They resist the lesbian and gay indifference to race which either has nothing to say about the matter or installs it as a possible variation on an otherwise self-identical sexuality. Notions of commonality and solidarity inherent in recent consolidations of the lesbian and gay community were severely challenged by the argument that race is at least as important as sexuality in defining group affiliations, personal identifications, and political strategies.

The increasingly organised articulation of the identities of lesbians and gays of colour destabilised the notion of a unitary gay identity. The assumptions that structured the core of the ethnic model of gay identity were similarly challenged and critiqued by non-normative sexualities. The ethnic model uncritically accepted dominant understandings of sexuality, figuring the sexual field through the binary opposition of heterosexuality and homosexuality. That is, it assumed it to be both self-evident and logical that sexual orientation is determined principally or even solely by the gender of one's sexual object choice. Sedgwick (1990:8) argues against the naturalisation of this system of classification:

> It is a rather amazing fact that, of the very many dimensions along which the genital activity of one person can be differentiated from that of another (dimensions that include preference for certain acts, certain zones or sensations, certain physical

types, a certain frequency, certain symbolic investments, certain relations of age or power, a certain species, a certain number of participants, etc. etc. etc.), precisely one, the gender of object choice, emerged from the turn of the century, and has remained, as *the* dimension denoted by the now ubiquitous category of 'sexual orientation'. (1990:8)

Pervasive

Although few proponents of those non-normative sexualities which found themselves further pathologised by the ethnic model of gay identity argued the point explicitly, debates in lesbian and gay circles during the late 1970s and early 1980s about bisexuality, sado-masochism, pornography, butch/fem, transvestism, prostitution and intergenerational sex implicitly questioned the hegemonic binarism of 'heterosexuality' and 'homosexuality'.

These debates about the validity of sexual variations took different forms in gay and lesbian feminist circles, each of which already constituted sexuality in a fundamentally different way. Gay and lesbian feminist debates were mutually informative. Yet relatively distinct understandings of sexuality were generated by the different principles and values of gay liberation and lesbian feminism. These discussions—so vehement at times that they have come to be known as the 'sex wars'—impacted most significantly on lesbian feminist circles, where lesbian sexuality had been theorised predominantly as a counter to masculine sexuality, which feminist analysis represented as overwhelmingly oppressive and objectifying. In some circles, where it had been recognised only recently as feminist, lesbianism became the quintessential manifestation of feminist sexuality. Theorised as a sexuality of equality untroubled by power differentials—and assumed to be about political choice and affectional preferences as much as about physical sex—lesbianism emerged almost by definition as the inverse of masculine sexuality. Lillian Faderman (1985:17–18) indicates the extent to which some lesbian feminists theorised lesbianism independently of sexuality:

Love between women has been primarily a sexual phenomenon only in male fantasy literature. 'Lesbian' describes a relationship in which two women's strongest emotions and affections are directed toward each other. Sexual contact may be a part of the relationship to a greater or lesser degree, or it may be entirely absent. By preference the two women spend most of their time together and share most aspects of their lives with each other.

Increasingly, there were challenges to the dominant lesbian feminist assumption that lesbian sex was couple-based, monogamous, woman-identified and political. Seeing that gay liberation had long recognised and valued a relatively wide range of sexual variation, similar debates on that issue were less energised although not without consequence.

Lesbian feminism has generally argued that exceptions to the 'standard' forms of lesbian sexuality—such as bisexuality, sadomasochism or butch/fem—are ideologically suspect assimilations of patriarchal values. Bisexual women are thus lesbians who maintain their heterosexual privilege instead of identifying fully with a devalued social identity: '[they are] pre-genderized, polymorphously perverse, or simply sexually undecided, uncommitted, and hence untrustworthy' (Daümer, 1992:92). Lesbians who identify as butch or fem belong to a pre-feminist era of lesbianism and consequently are thought to be either heroic or tragic, having internalised the heterosexual necessity for gender differentiation within a sexual relationship (Nestle, 1988). Sado-masochists are similarly understood to have internalised the eroticisation of cruelty and power imbalance that allegedly structures heterosexual relations. According to Sheila Jeffreys (1993:179), sadomasochism is both an immature form of sexuality and a consequence of 'the way in which sexuality under male supremacy is structured in individuals':

> Many lesbians have difficulty learning the correct female response of submissive sexual docility to men, but nevertheless we do not easily emerge unscathed from the construction of female sexuality around sadomasochism. Where we live under oppression and where there is virtually no escape for us, at least until we reach an advanced age, toward egalitarian relationships in which we take sexual initiatives, we have little alternative but to take pleasure from our oppression. The most common response is to eroticise our powerlessness in

masochism. For some women who see this as too 'effeminate' the role of humiliating women can be eroticised in sadism—the models for this in a woman-hating culture are everywhere.

When women who identified with these marginalised sexual categories began to assert their own identity-based demands for recognition, they undermined the hegemony of that 'standard' lesbian feminist sexuality which dissident groups characterised increasingly as asexual, dishonest and regulatory.

Similar skirmishes over the 'proper' delimitations of lesbian sexuality took place in the early 1980s in the United States, Canada, the United Kingdom, New Zealand and Australia. The general outlines of the debate are represented conveniently in a controversial conference held at Barnard College in 1982, and entitled 'Towards A Politics of Sexuality'. Two years later its proceedings were published as *Pleasure and Danger: Exploring Female Sexuality*. This book has quickly become a classic feminist text whose influence continues to be felt outside the North American context (Vance, 1984). Its title characterises feminist ambivalence about how to represent sexuality. *Pleasure and Danger* articulates many of the disquiets or dissatisfactions generated by the normative model of lesbian sexuality, and demonstrates Jeffrey Weeks's contention that 'sexual difference is a fragile bond for political identification' (1985:193).

Dorothy Allison (1984:111, 112) writes about her frustration that even within feminism, a movement which 'developed a major analysis around the issue of silence', certain sexual desires— namely 's/m, butch/femme, fetishes'—remain unspeakable. Joan Nestle (1984:234) challenges lesbian feminist authority by pointing to a different but disavowed genealogy, which includes butch/fem role-playing:

Questions and answers about lesbian lives that deviate from the feminist model of the 1970s strike like a shock wave against the movement's foundation, yet this new wave of questioning is an authentic one, coming from women who have helped create the feminist and lesbian movement that they are now challenging into new growth.

In a co-authored essay, Esther Newton and Shirley Walton—who identify themselves respectively as lesbian and heterosexual— argue that although binarised categories of sexual preference appear to be exhaustive, they need to be complicated and prolif- erated through a careful attention to other axes of sexual differen- tiation, which might include erotic identities, erotic roles and erotic acts (Newton and Walton, 1984). The tentative tone of this early collection indicates that what such speculations about the nature of lesbian sexuality imply is still being considered. Nevertheless, when Vance (1984:19) suggests in her introduction that 'sexual orientation is not the only, and may not be the most significant, sexual difference among women', she articulates a position that challenges the authority of the conventional lesbian feminist model of sexuality. For it follows from Vance's argument that sexual orientation may not constitute sufficient grounds for commonality among lesbians.

In an essay published a year after the 'Towards a Politics of Sexuality' conference, Pat Califia anticipates the logical extreme of Vance's argument when she observes that a primary identification as a sado-masochist can cut across and invalidate traditional descriptions of sexual orientation which regard the sex of one's object choice as definitive. Consequently, she argues that 'lesbian' —like 'gay man' or 'heterosexual'—is limited as a category of sex- ual identification. Califia (1983:26) finds it 'very odd that sexual orientation is defined solely in terms of the sex of one's partners', given that some sado-masochist sexual practices transgress the allegedly inviolate line between gay men and lesbians. 'I have sex with faggots', she writes. 'And I'm a lesbian' (ibid.:24). Describing her initiation into the mixed sado-masochistic scene, Califia out- lines a range of sexual practices that cannot be accommodated in traditional categories of sexual preference because they 'allow people to step outside the usually rigid boundaries of sexual orientation' (ibid.:25). Instead of abandoning traditional cate- gories, however, Califia continues to rearticulate them in scan- dalously different contexts:

> These combined experiences have resulted in a lifestyle that doesn't fit the homosexual stereotype. I live with my woman lover of five years. I have lots of casual sex with women. Once

in a while, I have casual sex with gay men. I have a three-year relationship with a homosexual man who doesn't use the term gay. And I call myself a lesbian. (ibid.)

Moreover, and indifferent to common-sense understandings, Califia maintains 'lesbian' as a category of personal identification. She does so not because (as might be expected) she is sexually attracted only to women, but because her lesbianism provides the context in which her sex acts with gay men are meaningful. 'I have eroticized queerness, gayness, homosexuality—in men or women', she writes. 'Sex with men outside the context of the gay community doesn't interest me at all. In a funny way, when two gay people of opposite sexes make it, it's still gay sex' (ibid.).

Such arguments were made strenuously and explicitly in the early 1990s by lesbians who were more interested in demonstrating the necessary limitations of identificatory categories than in broadening the definition of 'lesbian' in order to accommodate their own sexual preferences. In an essay wryly entitled 'My Interesting Condition', Jan Clausen (1990:12)—once a prominent lesbian activist and author with an international literary reputation—gives an account of her decision to become 'passionately involved with a man' after being in a monogamous lesbian relationship that lasted for twelve years. Discussing the confusion—both personal and collective—that this generated for a life-style and a community held together by identity politics, Clausen thinks that 'this experience . . . casts a novel and potentially valuable light on lesbian identity as it has been constructed by lesbian-feminists over the past two decades' (ibid.:13). Although she accounts for her behaviour largely in individualistic terms—such as personal needs and volitions, and specific circumstances—she still finds the conventional categories of identity problematic. While conceding that an identity politics makes possible certain structures and knowledges which to some extent are both sustaining and productive, Clausen questions the level of investment that lesbian feminism has in identity:

I do not want to become an identity junkie, hooked on the rush that comes with pinning down the essential characteristic that, for the moment, seems to offer the ultimate definition of the self, the quintessence of oppression, the locus of personal value—only to be superseded by the next revelation. (ibid.:17)

Instead of demanding that the category 'lesbian' should be broadened so as to represent her sexuality, Clausen suggests that its inability to do so—its representation of her sexual trajectory as treacherous or misguided—demonstrates its limitations; that is, the necessary limitations of identity politics.

Like Vance and Califia, Clausen implicitly questions the culturally dominant imperative to understand sexuality categorically in terms of sexual object choice. She critiques lesbian feminism for replicating that imperative as if it were somehow authentic in itself. 'When we assume lesbian identity to be unambiguous', writes Clausen (ibid.:19), 'when we are dismayed to discover attractions to men co-existing with women-loving, we reinscribe in a different form a prevailing, cultural myth about sexuality'. Moreover, she questions the assumed mutual exclusiveness of heterosexuality and homosexuality and understands bisexuality not as a taxonomic solution to her impasse but as an identity that is not one, an identity that undermines the foundations of identity politics: 'bisexuality is not a sexual identity at all, but a sort of anti-identity, a refusal (not, of course, conscious) to be limited to one object of desire, one way of loving' (ibid.:19).

There is ample evidence in a recent anthology, *Bi Any Other Name* (Hutchins and Kaahumanu, 1991), that, for some people, bisexuality complicates heterosexuality and homosexuality only in so far as it demands recognition as a third reified category. For others, like Clausen, however, bisexuality questions the role played by gender in defining sexual preference. Elizabeth Däumer (1992:95–6) develops such an argument when she suggests that it is not enough to install bisexuality as 'a sign of integration' between 'two mutually exclusive sexual cultures' and proposes instead that:

we assume bisexuality, not as an identity that integrates heterosexual and homosexual orientations, but as an epistemological as well as ethical vantage point from which we can examine and deconstruct the bipolar framework of gender and sexuality in which, as lesbians and lesbian feminists, we are still too deeply rooted, both because of and despite our struggle against homophobia and sexism.

Since 'the bipolar framework of gender and sexuality' is politically unproductive, bisexuality provides in Daümer's theory a point of critical leverage, a means of denaturalising that entire sex/gender system which stabilises not only heterosexuality but current understandings of lesbian feminism.

The intensity of these debates within lesbian feminism is not replicated within the related debates within gay liberationist or even ethnic models of gay identity. One reason for this is that an acceptance of sexual variation was already a constituent aspect of the gay male identity. Although valued differently in terms of community legitimation, gay sexual practices already recognised those rituals, styles and identifications that comprise monogamous and non-monogamous, private and public, couple and group, recreational and commercial sex. Nevertheless, there did indeed emerge 'a dominant, intimate norm' which, while tolerant of sexual diversity, was the focus of much heated debate about sado-masochism and intergenerational sex (Seidman, 1993a:124). The debates about sado-masochism were similar in both gay and lesbian communities but the debates about intergenerational sex had no substantially articulated counterpart in lesbian feminist circles, and consequently they are often understood by definition as not being feminist.

Variously referred to as intergenerational sex, child abuse, man–boy love and paedophilia, even the semantic continuum of terms used to describe the concept evokes a variety of positions in a debate structured overwhelmingly by such issues as consent, power and the legal definition of childhood. The association of paedophiles with gay men persists (in spite of evidence to the contrary) in homophobic culture, which is doubtless why the mainstream gay movement would be reluctant to countenance any official discussion of this matter. But the issue of intergenerational sex continues to be debated vigorously in many gay and lesbian communities. The protection of children is deemed by some to be ethically crucial to the development of gay identity, but is dismissed by others as 'erotic hysteria' (Rubin, 1993:6). What is the status of different, and arbitrary, age-of-consent laws? Do children have a sexuality and a right to sexual agency? Why is age—unlike, say, race or class—understood as a sexualised power-differential protected by law? Is it possible to eroticise children in an ethical way? These are questions commonly raised—and by no means yet resolved—in the controversy over intergenerational sex (cf. Altman, 1982:198–202; Weeks, 1985:223–31).

An initial response to the successful consolidation of gay and lesbian identities in the ethnic model was a demand for equal recognition of non-normative categories of identity. In certain cases, this developed into a dissatisfaction with the categories of identification themselves and a questioning of their efficacy in political intervention. 'Instead of assuming that collective identities simply reflect differences among persons that exist prior to mobilization', writes Stein (1991:36), 'we need . . . to look closely at the process by which movements remake identities'. It is not simply that 'the mobilization of homosexuals has provided a repertoire of ideology and organizational technology to other erotic populations', but rather that the increasing materialisation of those other erotic populations problematises the seemingly self-evident status of homosexuality as a category (Rubin, 1981:195). The suspicion that normative models of identity will never suffice for the representational work demanded of them is strengthened by influential postmodern understandings of identity, gender, sexuality, power and resistance. These provide the context in which queer becomes an intelligible—almost, one might say, an inevitable—phenomenon.

7

Queer

Homosexual, lesbian or gay, queer

Although the widespread use of 'queer' as a term of self-description is a relatively recent phenomenon, it is only the most recent in a series of words that have constituted the semantic forcefield of homosexuality since the nineteenth century. The word 'homosexuality'—coined in 1869 by a Swiss doctor, Karoly Maria Benkert—was not used widely in English until the 1890s, when it was adopted by the sexologist Havelock Ellis. It continues to have a certain currency but, because of its unshakeable association with the pathologising discourses of medicine, it is seldom used nowadays as a term of self-identification. 'To describe oneself as "a homosexual"', writes Simon Watney (1992:20), 'is immediately to inhabit a pseudo-scientific theory of sexuality which more properly belongs to the age of the steam engine than to the late twentieth century'.

More recently, in the 1960s, liberationists made a strategic break with 'homosexuality' by annexing the word 'gay', thus redeploying a nineteenth-century slang term which had formerly described women of dubious morals. 'Gay' was mobilised as a specifically political counter to that binarised and hierarchised sexual categorisation which classifies homosexuality as a deviation from a privileged and naturalised heterosexuality. Much conservative—not to mention linguistically naive—criticism was levelled at this appropriation on the grounds that an 'innocent' word was being 'perverted' from its proper usage. When John Boswell's book, *Christianity, Social Tolerance, and Homosexuality: Gay People in Western Europe from the Beginning of the Christian Era to the Fourteenth Century*, was published, Keith Thomas chided the publisher for allowing such slackness in Boswell's use of 'gay': 'History suggests that attempts to resist semantic change are almost invariably unsuccessful', he wrote. 'But it seems a pity that the University of Chicago Press should in this case have capitulated so readily' (1980:26). Thomas then specified what is wrong with this usage:

> The first objection is political. A minority is doubtless entitled to rebaptise itself with a term carrying more favourable connotations so as to validate its own behavior and free itself from scandal. But it is scarcely entitled to expect those who do not belong to that minority to observe this new usage, particularly when the chosen label seems bizarrely inappropriate and appears to involve an implicit slur upon everyone else . . . The second objection to 'gay' is linguistic. For centuries the word has meant (approximately) 'blithe,' 'light-hearted,' or 'exuberantly cheerful.' To endow it with a wholly different meaning is to deprive ourselves of a hitherto indispensable piece of vocabulary and incidentally to make nonsense of much inherited literature. (ibid.)

Only fifteen years later Thomas's objections seem comic. His outrage that 'gay' not only misdescribes homosexuals but also disenfranchises heterosexuals from such categorical happiness has been no more persuasive than his anxiety that the homonymous 'gay' would damage language and literature. Indeed, the popularity of the term 'gay' testifies to its potential as a non-clinical descriptor unburdened by the pathologising history of sexology.

Tracing etymological evolution is more commonly a general than a precise task. While, to a large extent, the terms 'homosexual', 'gay' or 'lesbian' and 'queer' successively trace historical shifts in the conceptualisation of same-sex sex, their actual deployment has sometimes been less predictable, often preceding or post-dating the periods which they respectively characterise. For example, George Chauncey (1994) observes that in the various subcultures which constituted the visible and complex gay world of pre-World War II New York the term 'queer' pre-dated 'gay'. He notes that 'by the 1910s and 1920s, men who identified themselves as different from other men primarily on the basis of their homosexual interest rather than their womanlike gender status usually called themselves "queer"' (Chauncey, 1994:101). By contrast, the term 'gay' first 'began to catch on in the 1930s, and its primacy was consolidated during the war' (ibid.:19). As recently as 1990 the *Encyclopedia of Homosexuality* glossed 'queer' as an almost archaic term, concluding—prematurely, as it turned out—that 'the word's declining popularity may therefore reflect today's greater visibility and acceptance of gay men and lesbians and the growing knowledge that most of them are in fact quite harmless, ordinary people' (Dynes, 1990:1091). While conceding that in twentieth-century America 'queer' 'has probably been the most popular vernacular term of abuse for homosexuals', the *Encyclopedia* incredulously reports that 'even today some older English homosexuals prefer the term, even sometimes affecting to believe that it is value-free' (ibid.). The examples of Chauncey and Dynes stand as cautionary reminders that the vagaries of historical evolution rarely match the altogether neater paradigms that purport to describe them. Nevertheless, the path traced by 'homosexual', 'gay' or 'lesbian' and 'queer' accurately describes the terms and identificatory categories commonly used to frame same-sex desire in the twentieth century.

Although these terms are clearly related to one another, the constructionist arguments surveyed in Chapter 2 indicate that they are not merely different ways of saying the same thing, and therefore should not be misrecognised as synonyms. As Simon Watney (1992:20) has argued: 'Far from being trivial issues, such questions of change and contestation at the level of intimate personal identities are fundamental to our understanding of the workings of power within the wider framework of Modernity'. 'Queer' is not simply the latest example in a series of words that describe and constitute same-sex desire transhistorically but rather a consequence of the constructionist problematising of any allegedly universal term. Noting in the recent discursive proliferation of lesbian and gay studies a certain hesitancy or self-consciousness about what terms to use in which circumstances, James Davidson (1994:12) writes: '*Queer* is in fact the most common solution to this modern crisis of utterance, a word so well-travelled it is equally at home in 19th-century drawing-rooms, accommodating itself to whispered insinuation, and on the streets of the Nineties, where it raises its profile to that of an empowering slogan'. In its erratic claims to various historic periods, Davidson argues that queer 'produces nothing but confusion' (ibid.). The critical term 'queer' has proved to have a highly elastic sense of history (see Chapter 1). But it has been most commonly mobilised not as a retrospective and transhistoricising descriptor, but as a term that indexes precisely and specifically cultural formations of the late 1980s and 1990s. Describing the shift from 'homosexual' to 'gay', Weeks (1977:3) argues that these terms 'are not just new labels for old realities: they point to a changing reality, both in the ways a hostile society labelled homosexuality, and in the way those stigmatized saw themselves'. Similarly, in distinguishing itself from those terms which form its semantic history, 'queer' equally foregrounds 'a changing reality' whose dimensions will now be examined further.

The post-structuralist context of queer

Queer marks both a continuity and a break with previous gay liberationist and lesbian feminist models. Lesbian feminist models of organisation were correctives to the masculinist bias of a gay liberation which itself had grown out of dissatisfactions with earlier homophile organisations. Similarly, queer effects a rupture which, far from being absolute, is meaningful only in the context of its historical development. The mock-historical sweep of gay evolution by Susan Hayes (1994:14) casts queer as the latest in a series of related events:

First there was Sappho (the good old days). Then there was the acceptable homoeroticism of classical Greece, the excesses of Rome. Then, casually to skip two millennia, there was Oscar Wilde, sodomy, blackmail and imprisonment, Forster, Sackville-West, Radclyffe Hall, inversion, censorship; then pansies, butch and femme, poofs, queens, fag hags, more censorship and blackmail, and Orton. Then there was Stonewall (1969) and we all became gay. There was feminism, too, and some of us became lesbian feminists and even lesbian separatists. There was drag and clones and dykes and politics and Gay Sweatshop. Then there was Aids, which, through the intense discussion of sexual practices (as opposed to sexual identities), spawned the Queer movement in America. Then that supreme manifestation of Thatcherite paranoia, Clause 28, which provoked the shotgun marriage of lesbian and gay politics in the UK. The child is Queer, and a problem child it surely is.

Although this account is too tongue-in-cheek to be a wholly persuasive genealogy of queer as a category, its parodic invocation of historical cause and effect certainly dramatises the ambivalent continuities and discontinuities that characterise queer's evolution.

While the mobilisation of queer in its most recent sense cannot be dated exactly, it is generally understood to have been popularly adopted in the early 1990s. Queer is a product of specific cultural and theoretical pressures which increasingly structured debates (both within and outside the academy) about questions of lesbian and gay identity. Perhaps most significant in this regard has been the problematising by post-structuralism of gay liberationist and lesbian feminist understandings of identity and the operations of power. This prompts David Herkt (1995:46) to argue that 'the Gay identity is observably a philosophically conservative construct, based upon premises that no longer have any persuasive academic relationship to contemporary theories of identity or gender'. The delegitimation of liberal, liberationist, ethnic and even separatist notions of identity generated the cultural space necessary for the emergence of the term 'queer'; its non-specificity guarantees it against recent criticisms made of the exclusionist tendencies of 'lesbian' and 'gay' as identity categories. Although there is no agreement on the exact definition of queer, the interdependent spheres of activism and theory that constitute its necessary context have undergone various shifts.

Before considering specific debates about the efficacy of queer, it is important to understand that those models of identity, gender and sexuality which in large part underwrite the queer agenda have changed, and to recognise the implications such changes have for the theorising of power and resistance. In distinguishing the Gay Liberation Front from Queer Nation, Joseph Bristow and Angelia R. Wilson (1993:1–2) consider it definitionally significant that 'an ertswhile politics of identity has largely been superseded by a politics of difference'. Similarly, Lisa Duggan (1992:15) notes that in queer models 'the rhetoric of difference replaces the more assimilationist liberal emphasis on similarity to other groups'. In identifying difference as a crucial term for queer knowledges and modes of organisation, these theorists map a change which is not specific to queer but characteristic of post-structuralism in general. As Donald Morton (1995:370) writes:

> Rather than as a local effect, the return of the queer has to be understood as the result, in the domain of sexuality, of the (post)modern encounter with—and rejection of—Enlighten-ment views concerning the role of the conceptual, rational, systematic, structural, normative, progressive, liberatory, revo-lutionary, and so forth, in social change.

Indeed, as an intellectual model, queer has not been produced solely by lesbian and gay politics and theory, but rather informed by historically specific knowledges which constitute late twentieth-century western thought. Similar shifts can be seen in both femi-nist and post-colonial theory and practice when, for example, Denise Riley (1988) problematises feminism's insistence on 'women' as a unified, stable and coherent category, and Henry Louis Gates (1985) denaturalises 'race'. Such conceptual shifts have had great impact within lesbian and gay scholarship and activism and are the historical context for any analysis of queer.

Both the lesbian and gay movements were committed funda-mentally to the notion of identity politics in assuming identity as the necessary prerequisite for effective political intervention. Queer, on the other hand, exemplifies a more mediated relation to categories of identification. Access to the post-structuralist theori-sation of identity as provisional and contingent, coupled with a growing awareness of the limitations of identity categories in terms of political representation, enabled queer to emerge as a new form of personal identification and political organisation. 'Identity' is probably one of the most naturalised cultural categories each of us inhabits: one always thinks of one's *self* as existing outside all representational frames, and as somehow marking a point of undeniable realness. In the second half of the twentieth century, however, such seemingly self-evident or logical claims to identity have been problematised radically on a number of fronts by such theorists as Louis Althusser, Sigmund Freud, Ferdinand de Saussure, Jacques Lacan and Michel Foucault. Collectively, their work has made possible certain advances in social theory and the human sciences which, in the words of Stuart Hall (1994:120), have effected 'the final de-centring of the Cartesian subject' (cf. Chris Weedon, 1987; Diana Fuss, 1989; Barbara Creed, 1994). Consequently, identity has been reconceptualised as a sustaining and persistent cultural fantasy or myth. To think of identity as a 'mythological' construction is not to say that categories of identity have no material effect. Rather it is to realise—as Roland Barthes does in his *Mythologies* (1978)—that our understanding of ourselves as coherent, unified, and self-determining subjects is an effect of those representational codes commonly used to describe the self and through which, consequently, identity comes to be understood. Barthes' understanding of subjectivity questions that seemingly natural or self-evident 'truth' of identity which derives historically from René Descartes' notion of the self as something that is self-determining, rational and coherent.

Reconsidering Karl Marx's emphasis on the framework of constraints or historical conditions which determine an individual's actions, Louis Althusser has argued that we do not pre-exist as free subjects: on the contrary, we are constituted as such by ideology. His central thesis is that individuals are 'interpellated' or 'called forth' as subjects by ideology, and that interpellation is achieved through a compelling mixture of recognition and identification. This notion is important for any thorough examination of identity politics, because it demonstrates how ideology not only positions individuals in society but also confers on them their sense of identity. In other words, it shows how one's identity is already constituted by ideology itself rather than simply by resistance to it.

Like the Marxist structuralist approach to subjectivity, psychoanalysis makes culturally available a narrative that complicates the assumption that an identity is the natural property of any individual. Sigmund Freud's theorisation of the unconscious further challenges the notion that subjectivity is stable and coherent. In establishing the formative influence of important mental and psychic processes of which an individual is unaware, the theory of the unconscious has radical implications for the common-sense assumption that the subject is both whole and self-knowing. Furthermore, interpretations of Freud's work—particularly by the French psychoanalyst, Jacques Lacan—establish subjectivity as something which must be learned, rather than as something which is always already there. Subjectivity is not an essential property of the self, but something which originates outside it. Identity, then, is an effect of identification with and against others: being ongoing, and always incomplete, it is a process rather than a property.

In some influential lectures on structural linguistics which he delivered in 1906–11, Ferdinand de Saussure argues that language does not so much reflect as construct social reality. For Saussure, language is not some second-order system whose function is simply to describe what is already there. Rather, language constitutes and makes significant that which it seems only to describe. Moreover, Saussure defines language as a system of signification that precedes any individual speaker. Language is commonly misunderstood as the medium by which we express our 'authentic' selves, and our private thoughts and emotions. Saussure, however, asks us to consider that our notions of a private, personal and interior self is something constituted through language.

The theories of Althusser, Freud, Lacan and Saussure provide the post-structuralist context in which queer emerges. The French historian Michel Foucault has been more explicitly engaged in denaturalising dominant understandings of sexual identity. In emphasising that sexuality is not an essentially personal attribute but an available cultural category—and that it is the effect of power rather than simply its object—Foucault's writings have been crucially significant for the development of lesbian and gay and, subsequently, queer activism and scholarship. To say this is not to claim that there is literally a causal connection between Foucault's work and queer practice and theory. Yet, as Diana Fuss (1989:97) observes, Foucault's work on sexuality resonates with 'current disputes amongst gay theorists and activists over the meaning and applicability of such categories as "gay", "lesbian", and "homosexual" in a post-structuralist climate which renders all such assertions of identity problematic'.[1]

Foucault's argument that sexuality is a discursive production rather than a natural condition is part of his larger contention that modern subjectivity is an effect of networks of power. Not only negative or repressive but also productive and enabling, power is 'exercised from innumerable points' to no predetermined effect (Foucault, 1981:94). Against the popular concept that sex both exists beyond power relations and yet is repressed by them, Foucault (1979:36) argues that power is not primarily a repressive force:

> In defining the effects of power by repression, one accepts a purely juridical conception of that power; one identifies power with a law that says no; it has above all the force of an interdict. Now, I believe that this is a wholly negative, narrow and skeletal conception of power which has been curiously shared. If power was never anything but repressive, if it never did anything but say no, do you really believe that we should manage to obey it? What gives power its hold, what makes it accepted, is quite simply the fact that it does not simply weigh like a force which says no, but that it runs through, and it produces, things, it induces pleasure, it forms knowledge, it produces discourse; it must be considered as a productive network which runs through the entire social body much more than as a negative instance whose function is repression.

In Foucault's analysis, marginalised sexual identities are not simply victims of the operations of power. On the contrary, they are produced by those same operations: 'For two centuries now, the discourse on sex has been multiplied rather than rarefied; and if it has carried with it taboos and prohibitions, it has also, in a more fundamental way, ensured the solidification and implantation of an entire sexual mosaic' (Foucault, 1981:53). This emphasis on the productive and enabling aspects of power profoundly alters the models by which traditionally it has been understood. Consequently, Foucault's revaluation of power has significantly affected much lesbian and gay analysis.

Since he does not think that power is a fundamentally repressive force, Foucault does not endorse such liberationist strategies as breaking prohibitions and speaking out. Indeed, because the idea of modern sexual repression is widely accepted, Foucault speculates that the discursive critique of oppression, far from correctly identifying the mechanisms of power, 'is . . . in fact part of the same historical network as the thing it denounces (and doubtless misrepresents) by calling it "repression"' (ibid.:10). Foucault questions the liberationist confidence that to voice previously denied and silenced lesbian and gay identities and sexualities is to defy power, and hence induce a transformative effect. As Foucault takes a resolutely anti-liberatory position on this matter he is sometimes read—perhaps unsurprisingly given the common currency of what he critiques as 'the repressive hypothesis'—as advocating political defeatism (ibid.:15).

Yet Foucault also argues that 'where there is power, there is resistance' (ibid.:95), a resistance 'coextensive with [power] and absolutely its contemporary' (Foucault, 1988:122). Like power, resistance is multiple and unstable; it coagulates at certain points, is dispersed across others, and circulates in discourse. 'Discourse' is the heterogeneous collection of utterances that relate to a particular concept, and thereby constitute and contest its meaning— that 'series of discontinuous segments whose tactical function is neither uniform nor stable' (ibid.:100). Just as he cautions against thinking that power demarcates only hierarchical relations, so Foucault insists that discourse is not simply for or against anything, but endlessly prolific and multivalent: 'we must not imagine a world of discourse divided between accepted discourse and excluded discourse, or between the dominant discourse and the dominated one; but as a multiplicity of discursive elements that can come into play in various strategies' (ibid.).

When describing the relation between discourses and strategies, and demonstrating how a single discourse can be used strategically for oppositional purposes, Foucault specifically instances how the category of homosexuality was formed in relation to structures of power and resistance. The rise of the homosexual as a 'species' exemplifies the polyvalent capacities of discourse:

> There is no question that the appearance in nineteenth-century psychiatry, jurisprudence, and literature of a whole series of discourses on the species and subspecies of homosexuality, inversion, pederasty, and 'psychic hermaphrodism' made possible a strong advance of social controls into this area of 'perversity'; but it also made possible the formation of a 'reverse' discourse: homosexuality began to speak in its own behalf, to demand that its legitimacy or 'naturality' be acknowledged, often in the same vocabulary, using the same categories by which it was medically disqualified. (ibid.:101)

Discourse, then, is entirely within (yet not necessarily in the service of) the mechanisms of power. Foucault's analysis focuses on discourse as a mode of resistance, not to contest its content but in order to particularise its strategic operations. In so far as homosexuality is one of his key examples, Foucault regards sexual identities as the discursive effects of available cultural categories. Challenging commonly held understandings of power and resistance, his work has obvious appeal for lesbian and gay—and subsequently queer—theory and practice. Although Foucault (1988b) treats the 'author' as a textual effect rather than a real presence, his public identity as a gay man may well have facilitated the gay studies inspired by his work.

Even more explicitly than Althusser, Saussure, Freud and Lacan, Foucault radically reconceptualises identity in ways that have substantially reshaped lesbian and gay studies. The recent critique of identity politics—both inside and outside lesbian and gay circles—has not arisen simply because the reification of any single identity is felt to be exclusionary. It has occurred because, within poststructuralism, the very notion of identity as a coherent and abiding sense of self is perceived as a cultural fantasy rather than a demonstrable fact. Objections to the emphasis on identity in lesbian and gay politics were based initially on the fact that the foundational category of any identity politics inevitably excludes potential subjects in the name of representation. Clearly, lesbian and gay identity politics that merely replicate race and class oppression are inadequate. Yet identity politics cannot be recovered simply by a scrupulous attention to the axes of difference. For as post-structuralism also demonstrates, identity politics are eviscerated not only by the differences *between* subjects but the irresolvable differences *within* each subject. As Diana Fuss (1989:103) argues, 'theories of "multiple identities" fail to challenge effectively the traditional metaphysical understanding of identity as unity'.

Performativity and identity

Within lesbian and gay studies, the theorist who has done most to unpack the risks and limits of identity is Judith Butler. In her wide-ly cited book, *Gender Trouble: Feminism and the Subversion of Identity* (1990), Butler elaborates Foucault's argument about the operations of power and resistance in order to demonstrate the ways in which marginalised identities are complicit with those identificatory regimes they seek to counter. If Foucault's *The History of Sexuality* (vol. 1) is for David Halperin (1995:15) 'the single most important intellectual source of political inspiration for contemporary AIDS activists', then for Eve Kosofsky Sedgwick (1993a:1) Butler's *Gender Trouble* is the correspondingly influen-tial book for queer theory: 'Anyone who was at the 1991 Rutgers conference on Gay and Lesbian Studies, and heard *Gender Trouble* appealed to in paper after paper, couldn't help being awed by the productive impact this dense and even imposing work has had on the recent development of queer theory and reading'. Rosemary Hennessy (1994:94) similarly reports that 'Judith Butler is cited more persistently and pervasively than any other queer theorist'. Although *Gender Trouble* is framed most prominently in terms of feminism, one of its most influential achievements is to specify how gender operates as a regulatory construct that privileges heterosexuality and, furthermore, how the deconstruction of normative models of gender legitimates lesbian and gay subject-positions.

Butler argues—controversially—that feminism works against its explicit aims if it takes 'women' as its grounding category. This is because the term 'women' does not signify a natural unity but instead a regulatory fiction, whose deployment inadvertently reproduces those normative relations between sex, gender and desire that naturalise heterosexuality. 'The cultural matrix through which gender identity has become intelligible', writes Butler (1990:17), 'requires that certain kinds of "identities" cannot "exist" —that is, those in which gender does not follow from sex and those in which the practices of desire do not "follow" from either sex or gender'. Instead of naturalising the same-sex desire of homosexuality—which is the usual strategy of gay and lesbian movements—Butler contests the truth of gender itself, arguing that any commitment to gender identity works ultimately against the legitimation of homosexual subjects.

No longer a natural basis for solidarity, gender is refigured by Butler as a cultural fiction, a performative effect of reiterative acts: 'Gender is the repeated stylization of the body, a set of repeated acts within a highly rigid regulatory frame that congeal over time to produce the appearance of substance, of a natural sort of being' (ibid.:33). Consequently, there is nothing authentic about gender, no 'core' that produces the reassuring signs of gender. The reason 'there is no gender identity behind the expressions of gender' is 'that identity is performatively constituted by the very "expressions" that are said to be its results' (ibid.:25). Heterosexuality, which passes itself off as natural and therefore in no need of explanation, is reframed by Butler as a discursive production, an effect of the sex/gender system which purports merely to describe it. Like Foucault, who foregrounds the importance of discursive strategies and their revisionist potential, Butler identifies gender as 'an ongoing discursive practice . . . open to intervention and resignification' (ibid.:33). Her strategic resignification of normative gender models and heterosexuality is achieved by staging gender in ways that emphasise the manner in which 'the "unity" of gender is the effect of a regulatory practice that seeks to render gender identity uniform through a compulsory heterosexuality' (ibid.:31).

'What kind of subversive repetition might call into question the regulatory practice of identity itself?' asks Butler (ibid.:32). She argues that those failures or confusions of gender—those performative repetitions that do not consolidate the law but that (remembering Foucault's emphasis on the productive aspects of power) are nevertheless generated by that law—highlight the discursive rather than the essential character of gender. Heterosexuality is naturalised by the performative repetition of normative gender identities. Butler advocates contesting such naturalisation by means of a displaced repetition of its performativity that would draw attention to those processes that consolidate sexual identities. One of the strategies she recommends is a parodic repetition of gender norms. Instead of marking a distance between itself and the parodied original, the kind of parody which Butler has in mind 'is *of* the very notion of an original' (ibid.:138). Consequently, heterosexuality is no longer assumed to be the original of which homosexuality is an inferior copy. In advocating parody as a resistant strategy, Butler intends to demonstrate that the domains of gender and sexuality are not organised in terms of originality and imitation. What they manifest instead is the endless—though heavily regulated—possibilities of performativity.

By persistently denaturalising gender and sexuality, Butler problematises many of the cherished assumptions of gay liberation and lesbian feminism, including their appeals to commonality and collectivity. Michael Warner (1992:19) points to discontinuities in their respective theoretical frames when he compares the Radicalesbian manifesto with Butler's work:

> Radicalesbians began their manifesto 'What is a lesbian? A lesbian is the rage of all women condensed to the point of explosion'. If Butler could be persuaded to regard the question 'What is a lesbian?' as one worth answering, she might respond that 'a lesbian is the incoherence of gender binarism and heterosexuality condensed to the point of parody'.

While Butler is interested in all performativities that repeat the law with a difference, she focuses on drag as a practice that reinflects heterosexual norms within a gay context:

> As much as drag creates a unified picture of "woman" . . . it also reveals the distinctness of those aspects of gendered experience which are falsely naturalized as a unity through the regulatory fiction of heterosexual coherence. *In imitating gender, drag implicitly reveals the imitative structure of gender itself—as well*

as its contingency. Indeed, part of the pleasure, the giddiness of the performance is in the recognition of a radical contingency in the relation between sex and gender in the face of cultural configurations of causal unities that are regularly assumed to be natural and necessary (Butler, 1990:137–8).

Butler does not consider drag to be an essentially subversive parody. Rather, in its literal staginess, it offers an effective cultural model for deconstructing those commonly held assumptions that privilege certain genders and sexualities by attributing 'natural-ness' and 'originality' to them. She argues just as emphatically— although, as subsequent uses of her work demonstrate, less mem-orably—for the efficacy of all those troublesome gender perfor-mances which 'repeat and displace through hyperbole, dissonance, internal confusion, and proliferation the very constructs by which they are mobilized' (ibid.:31).

Butler's notion of performativity has gone into a kind of hyper-circulation. Mentioned in passing here, pressed into more rigorous service there, it has been highly productive for lesbian and gay studies in the 1990s. Most commonly, however, critics who appro-priate Butler's notion of performativity literalise it as performance, and concentrate on those theatricalised stagings of gender which self-consciously interrogate the relations between sex, gender and desire. Performativity figures, for example, in the work of Judith Halberstam (1994) on female masculinity, Cathy Schwichtenberg (1993) on Madonna, and Paula Graham (1995) on the male lesbian and camp. While the concept of performativity includes these and other self-reflexive instances, equally—if less obviously—it explains those everyday productions of gender and sexual identi-ty which seem most to evade explanation. For gender is perfor-mative, not because it is something that the subject deliberately and playfully assumes, but because, through reiteration, it con-solidates the subject. In this respect, performativity is the precon-dition of the subject.

In a later book, *Bodies That Matter* (1993a), Butler puzzles over reductive uses of her work, and particularly the tendency to con-sider performativity literally and theatrically in terms of drag. Presented by Butler as an *example* of performativity, drag was

taken by many of her readers to be '*exemplary* of performativity';
as such, it satisfied 'the political needs of an emergent queer
movement in which the publicization of theatrical agency has
become quite central' (Butler, 1993a:231). Distancing herself from
those who understand gender as wilfully performed, Butler emphasises that 'performativity is neither free play nor theatrical self-
presentation; nor can it be simply equated with performance'
(ibid.:95). To counter these dominant misreadings of her work—
and to discourage thinking about performativity in voluntarist or
deliberate terms—Butler introduces the notions of 'constituted-
ness' and 'constraint':

> Performativity cannot be understood outside of a process of
> iterability, a regularized and constrained repetition of norms.
> And this repetition is not performed *by* a subject; this repetition
> is what enables a subject and constitutes the temporal condition
> for the subject. This iterability implies that 'performance' is not
> a singular 'act' or event, but a ritualized production, a ritual
> reiterated under and through constraint, under and through the
> force of prohibition and taboo, with the threat of ostracism and
> even death controlling and compelling the shape of the pro-
> duction, but not, I will insist, determining it fully in advance.
> (ibid.)

Butler reiterates the fact that gender, being performative, is not
like clothing, and therefore cannot be put on or off at will. Rather
it is constrained—not simply in the sense of being structured by
limitations but because (given the regulatory frameworks in which
performativity is meaningful) constraint is the prerequisite of performativity.

Although Butler carefully specifies her anti-voluntarist position—and emphasises that performativity is not something a subject *does*, but a process through which that subject is *constituted*—
her notion of performativity has been criticised as a naive render-
ing of more complex material conditions. Literalising Butler's
notion of performativity, Sheila Jeffreys (1994:461) misrepresents it
as a kind of quasi-theatricality, and not the register of everyday
gendered life. 'Surely it would be hard not to notice', she asks
rhetorically if also counter-intuitively, 'that a problem arises when

seeking to include lesbians in notions of camp and queer which depend on "performativity" of the feminine?' Jeffreys's problem, however, arises only when 'performativity' (in Butler's sense) is misunderstood as being a pretence and therefore less real than some underlying gender truth. Yet the theoretical significance of Butler's performativity is that *all gender*—and not simply that which self-consciously dramatises its theatricality—*is performative*. Since lesbians—no more nor less than any other group constituted as subjects through the repetition of gender norms— 'perform' gender, there is no problem in theorising lesbianism within models that depend on Butler's notion of performativity.

Jeffreys persists in misreading Butler despite the fact that her evidence comes from the very article in which Butler explicitly corrects such misapprehensions. Although Butler (1993b:21) specifically describes gender as 'performative insofar as it is the *effect* of a regulatory regime of gender differences in which genders are divided and hierarchised *under constraint*', Jeffreys (1993:81) maintains that Butler's understanding of gender is 'removed from a context of power relations'. Jeffreys also trivialises Butler's emphasis on the subversive potential of understanding gender performatively:

> When a woman is being beaten by the brutal man she lives with is this because she has adopted the feminine gender in her appearance? Would it be a solution for her to adopt a masculine gender for the day and strut about in a work shirt or leather chaps? (ibid.)

Clearly, the answer—for Butler as for Jeffreys—is no. It is worth noting—precisely because Jeffreys doesn't—that Butler (1993b:22) specifically argues that 'gender performativity is not a matter of choosing which gender one will be today'. Jeffreys ignores the anti-voluntarist emphasis of Butler's argument. Consequently, in criticising Butler's notion of performativity, Jeffreys not only oversimplifies Butler's theoretical position but also misrecognises her own over-simplification as a deficiency of the position she seeks to discredit.

In an essay which is more attentive to Butler's text and correspondingly more persuasive, Kath Weston also critiques Butler's emphasis on the performative. Although she considers aspects of performativity theory productive, Weston (1993:5) finds 'this framework inadequate to comprehend the complexities of the gendering of lesbian relationships'. Weston's criticisms, however, depend again on a misreading of performativity as a voluntary theatricality. Concluding that performativity falls short of 'its promise of a personal/political empowerment'—as well it might, since empowerment is not what performativity promises—Weston foregrounds what she takes to be inadequate about the performative understanding of gender by introducing the trope of the wardrobe. 'When a lesbian opens the closet door to put together an outfit for the evening', she writes, 'the size of her paycheck limits the choices she finds available' (ibid.:14). There is no disputing the accuracy of this observation. Yet to reduce Butler's understanding of performativity to the closet—to clothes, and the seemingly endless possibility of assuming and casting off gender identities—is a serious misreading. Weston's title—'Do Clothes Make the Woman?'—implies that, in a theory of performativity, they do. Yet Butler—in a passage fortuitously rendered in the same vocabulary—emphatically states that they don't: 'The publication of *Gender Trouble* coincided with a number of publications that did assert that "clothes make the women", but I never did think that gender was like clothes, or that clothes make the woman' (Butler, 1993a:231).

While understanding that performativity is not 'the efficacious expression of a human will in language' (ibid.:187), Elizabeth Grosz (1994a:139) disputes the centralisation of gender in performativity on the grounds that 'gender *must* be understood as a kind of overlay on a pre-established foundation of sex—a cultural variation of a more or less fixed and universal substratum'. As a consequence of characterising gender in this way, Grosz argues that Butler's account of performativity ought to focus properly on sex: 'The force of [Butler's] already powerful arguments would, I believe, be strengthened, if instead of the play generated by a term somehow beyond the dimension of sex, in the order of gender, she focused on the instabilities of sex itself, of bodies themselves' (ibid.:140). Such a change in focus would denaturalise sex by drawing attention to the fact that 'there is an instability at the

very heart of sex and bodies, that the body is what it is capable of
doing, and what anybody is capable of doing is well beyond the
tolerance of any given culture' (ibid.). To recommend that sex—a
category that historically has been theorised as more 'natural' than
gender—be denaturalised is valuable. Yet Butler's project is closer
to her own than Grosz allows. For although Butler undeniably
prioritises gender, she does not, as Grosz suggests, mobilise it in
opposition to some more foundational sense of sex. On the contrary, she explicitly questions such a reification of sex:

> If the immutable character of sex is contested, perhaps this con-
> struct called 'sex' is as culturally constructed as gender; indeed,
> perhaps it was always already gender, with the consequence
> that the distinction between sex and gender turns out to be no
> distinction at all.
>
> It would make no sense, then, to define gender as the cul-
> tural interpretation of sex, if sex itself is a gendered category.
> Gender ought not to be conceived merely as the cultural
> inscription of meaning on a pregiven sex . . . [because it] must
> also designate the very apparatus of production whereby the
> sexes themselves are established (Butler, 1990:7).

In contesting the allegedly immutable character of sex, Butler
(ibid.:6–7) asks the following questions:

> And what is 'sex' anyway? Is it natural, anatomical, chromo-
> somal, or hormonal, and how is a feminist critic to assess the
> scientific discourses which purport to establish such 'facts' for
> us? Does sex have a history? Does each sex have a different his-
> tory, or histories? Is there a history of how the duality of sex
> was established, a genealogy that might expose the binary
> options as a variable construction? Are the ostensibly natural
> facts of sex discursively produced by various scientific dis-
> courses in the service of other political and social interests?

In refusing the commonly assumed distinction between sex and
gender, and in dismantling those allegedly causal relations that
structure the difference between the two, Butler—like Grosz—
foregrounds the 'instability at the very heart of sex'.

Debates about performativity put a denaturalising pressure on
sex, gender, sexuality, bodies and identities. In proliferating as an

explanatory model—and being subject to contestations and negotiations—performativity has engendered a renewed engagement
with those processes by which the identity categories we inhabit
determine our knowledge and everyday ways of being in the
world. Butler's rigorous deconstruction of identity is most evident
in lesbian and gay studies' cultivation of a suspicion about the effi-
cacies of identity, its 'crisis about "gay" identity' (Cohen, 1991:82).
In the wake of Butler's critique, homosexuality—like heterosexuality—comes to be understood as the effect of signifying practices,
an 'identity effect' that concentrates at certain bodies: '"Homosexual", like "woman", is not a name that refers to a "natural kind"
of thing', David Halperin explains (1995:45). 'It's a discursive, and
homophobic, construction that has come to be misrecognized as
an object under the epistemological regime known as realism.' As
a result of this profound suspicion of classification, identity categories have come to be considered complicit in the very structures
that their assertion was intended to overthrow. For Butler
(1991:13–14), 'identity categories tend to be instruments of regulatory regimes, whether as the normalizing categories of oppressive
structures or as the rallying points for a liberatory contestation of
that very oppression'. Formerly assumed to be a prerequisite for
political intervention, the assertion of collective identities is now
routinely understood to put into circulation effects in excess of its
avowed intention.

In stark contrast to those liberationist or ethnic gay and lesbian
models that affirm identity, promote 'coming out', and proclaim
homosexuality under the organising affect of 'pride', lesbian and
gay studies in the 1990s have begun to question and resist identity
categories and their promise of unity and political effectiveness.
That 'recognition of the precarious state of identity and a full
awareness of the complicated processes of identity formation,
both psychical and social' which Diana Fuss (1989:100) called for
in relation to gay and lesbian identity politics now commonly
undergirds queer practice and theory. Frequently the categories
'lesbian' and 'gay' are both interrogated and denaturalised even as
they are being mobilised in critical discourse and political practice.
Ed Cohen (1991:72) writes of his difficulty in identifying with the
category 'gay man' because he finds that term's implicit claims to
collectivity unpersuasive: 'By predicating "our" affinity upon the

assertion of a common "sexuality", we tacitly agree to leave unexplored any "internal" contradictions which undermine the coherence we desire from the imagined certainty of an unassailable commonality or of incontestable sexuality.' Similarly, Butler (1991:14) discusses her ambivalence about writing an essay for an anthology which, in being subtitled *Lesbian Theories, Gay Theories*, seems to identify her with the very terms she is contesting: 'I am skeptical about how the "I" is determined as it operates under the title of the lesbian sign, and I am no more comfortable with its homophobic determination than with those normative definitions offered by other members of the "gay or lesbian community"'. The strenuousness of these efforts to denaturalise such seemingly self-evident categories as 'identity' and 'sexuality' is discernible here in the diacritical work that both Butler and Cohen devolve to quotation marks: 'our', 'sexuality', 'I', 'gay and lesbian community'. The same strategy is employed relentlessly by Valerie Traub (1995), who always encloses the word 'lesbian' in quotation marks.

The widespread discontent with that version of identity politics which is advocated in both liberationist and ethnic models of homosexuality is generated not only by a sense of resistance to a new normativity but also by a more sophisticated understanding of the interworkings of identity and power, as evident in comments by David Halperin (1995:32):

Disenchantment with liberation [does not] proceed merely from a growing awareness that gay life has generated its own disciplinary regimes, its own techniques of normalization, in the form of obligatory haircuts, T-shirts, dietary practices, body piercing, leather accoutrements, and physical exercise ... Ultimately, I think, what the shift away from a liberation model of gay politics reflects is a deepened understanding of the discursive structures and representational systems that determine the production of sexual meanings, and that micromanage individual perceptions, in such a way as to maintain and reproduce the underpinnings of heterosexist privilege.

This 'deepened understanding' of how the marshalling of lesbian and gay identities might inadvertently reinforce that heterosexual hegemony they are programmatically opposed to has generated an imperative—even a willingness—to adopt analytical models that question the authenticity of identity, and particularly those that critique the putatively causal relation between a secure identity and an effective politics.

The implications of such a critique for lesbian and gay politics are taken up by Diana Fuss (1989:100) when she asks:

> Is politics based on identity, or is identity based on politics? Is identity a natural, political, historical, psychical, or linguistic construct? What implications does the deconstruction of 'identity' have for those who espouse an identity politics? Can feminist, gay, or lesbian subjects afford to dispense with the notion of unified, stable identities or must we begin to base our politics on something other than identity? What, in other words, is the politics of 'identity politics'?

Although queer was not a popular term of self-identification at the time when Fuss articulated these questions, its recent deployment is often informed by those issues of identity, community and politics that she raises here. A similar scrutinising of lesbian and gay identities can be seen in the queer engagement with post-structural critiques of subjectivity and individual or collective identities, its pragmatic crystallisation and deployment of recently reworked subject positions, and in its attention to the discursive formations of the various terms by which homosexuality in particular and sexuality more generally are categorised.

HIV/AIDS discourse

If post-structuralist theory can be claimed as part of the context of queer, then queer's emergence as a diacritical term can be linked just as plausibly to developments outside—but not discrete from—the academy. The most frequently cited context for queer in this sense is the network of activism and theory generated by the AIDS epidemic, parts of which have found that queer offers a rubric roomy and assertive enough for political intervention. In this respect, queer is understood as a response not only to 'the AIDS crisis [which] prompted a renewal of radical activism' (Seidman,

1994:172) but also to 'the growing homophobia brought about by public response to AIDS' (Creed, 1994:152). What set of effects—put into circulation around the AIDS epidemic—both necessitated and nurtured those new forms of political organisation, education, and theorising that are produced under the rubric of queer? An adequate answer to this question has to take account of the following:

- the ways in which the status of the subject or individual is problematised in the biomedical discourses which construct AIDS (Haraway, 1989)
- the shift—effected by safe-sex education—in emphasising sexual practices over sexual identities (Bartos et al., 1993:69–72; Dowsett, 1991:5)
- the persistent misrecognition of AIDS as a gay disease (Meyer, 1991:275) and of homosexuality as a kind of fatality (Hanson, 1991; Nunokawa, 1991:311–16)
- the coalitional politics of much AIDS activism that rethinks identity in terms of affinity rather than essence (Saalfield and Navarro, 1991) and therefore includes not only lesbians and gay men but also bisexuals, transsexuals, sex workers, PWAs (People with AIDS), health workers, and parents and friends of gays
- the pressing recognition that discourse is not a separate or second-order 'reality', and the consequent emphasis on contestation in resisting dominant depictions of HIV and AIDS and representing them otherwise (Edelman, 1994:79–92)
- the rethinking of traditional understandings of the workings of power in cross-hatched struggles over epidemiology, scientific research, public health, and immigration policy (Halperin, 1995:28).

These are just some of the multidirectional pressures which the AIDS epidemic places on categories of identification, power and knowledge. Their relation to the rise of queer as a potent and enabling term is more than coincidental.

While responses to the AIDS epidemic—governmental, medical, scientific, activist, theoretical—cannot be held entirely responsible for generating the conditions in which queer emerged

as a significant term, the urgent need to resist dominant constructions of HIV/AIDS reinforced a radical revision of contemporary
lesbian and gay politics. Commenting on the historical failures or
limitations of the gay and lesbian movements—such as inadequate
attention to internal differences, and an inability to collaborate effectively with other liberation movements—Douglas Crimp (1993:
314) writes: 'The AIDS crisis brought us face-to-face with the consequences of both our separatism and our liberalism. And it is in
this new political conjuncture that the word "queer" has been
reclaimed to designate new political identities'. The 'new political
identities' enabled by queer are very often intent on denaturalising
those categories which AIDS renders equally strange. Like queer,
observes Thomas Yingling (1991:292),

> the material effects of AIDS deplete so many of our cultural
> assumptions about identity, justice, desire, and knowledge that
> it seems at times able to threaten the entire system of Western
> thought—that which maintains the health and immunity of our
> epistemology: the psychic presence of AIDS signifies a collapse
> of identity and difference that refuses to be abjected from the
> systems of self-knowledge.

A similar recognition of the 'collapse of identity and difference'
prompts Lee Edelman (1994:96) to argue that queer and AIDS are
interconnected, because each is articulated through a post-
modernist understanding of the death of the subject, and both
understand identity as a curiously ambivalent site: '"AIDS", then,
can be figured as a crisis in—and hence an opportunity for—the
social shaping or articulation of subjectivities'. In so far as AIDS
enables—and at times, demands—a radical rethinking of the cultural and psychic constitution of subjectivity itself, Edelman finds
in it the promise of a refashioned subjectivity, which might rearticulate current notions not only of identity but also of politics,
community and agency:

> we have the chance to displace that [oppressive] logic [of
> the culture] and begin to articulate the range of options for
> what might *become* a postmodern subject; we have the chance,
> in other words, to challenge, as Andreas Huyssen suggests

postmodernism must, '*the ideology of the subject* (as male, white, and middle-class [and we must add, as he does not, heterosexual]) by developing alternative and different notions of subjectivity. (ibid.:111)

Perhaps not surprisingly in this context, Edelman concludes that 'such a mutation of the gay subject can already be seen in the process by which, in certain quarters, "gay" is being rewritten as "queer"' (ibid.:113).

The most public mobilisations of the term 'queer' have doubtless been in the services of AIDS activism, which in turn has been one of the most visible sites for the restructuring of sexual identities. The relationship between the new and decentralised activism, and the coming into prominence of queer as a term that can direct attention to identity without solidifying it is contextual rather than causal. Certainly debates (in what were once lesbian and gay contexts) about how to refigure subjectivities and identities differently have been partly reinforced and partly provoked by the new urgency generated by the AIDS crisis. Yet such debates about identity and the most efficacious ways of ensuring social transformation have been equally, if less spectacularly, energised by developments in post-structuralist, feminist and post-colonial circles. All of these have challenged the notion of a stable identity— not simply because it is a fiction but because it is the sort of fiction which may well work against the interests of those constituents it claims to represent.

Queer identity

Given the extent of its commitment to denaturalisation, queer itself can have neither a foundational logic nor a consistent set of characteristics: '*There is nothing in particular to which it necessarily refers*', writes David Halperin (1995:62, original emphasis). 'It is an identity without an essence.' This fundamental indeterminacy makes queer a difficult object of study; always ambiguous, always relational, it has been described as 'a largely intuitive and half-articulate theory' (Warner, 1992:19). Queer's ambiguity is often cited as the reason for its mobilisation. Defining queer as a term which 'mark[s] a flexible space for the expression of all aspects of non- (anti-, contra-) straight cultural production and reception', Alexander Doty (1993:3, 2) finds it attractive in so far as he also wants 'to find a term with some ambiguity, a term that would describe a wide range of impulses and cultural expressions, including space for describing and expressing bisexual, transsexual, and straight queerness'. Queer is widely perceived as calling into question conventional understandings of sexual identity by deconstructing the categories, oppositions and equations that sustain them (Hennessy, 1994:94); yet 'just what "queer" signifies or includes or refers to is by no means easy to say' (Abelove, 1993:20). Partly because queer is necessarily indeterminate, Sedgwick argues in a recent interview that calling yourself queer 'dramatises the difference between what you call yourself and what other people call you. There is a sense in which queer can only be used in the first person' (Hodges, 1994). Sedgwick's provocative suggestion that, despite its routine circulation as a descriptive term, queer can only be auto-descriptive emphasises the extent to which queer refers to self-identification rather than to empirical observations of other people's characteristics.

Even more than the lesbian and gay models from which it has developed, queer evades programmatic description, because it is differently valued in different contexts. Often used as a convenient shorthand for the more ponderous 'lesbian and gay', 'queer' is a boon to sub-editors. Gay and lesbian community newspapers evidence an enthusiasm for 'queer' as the preferred synonym for 'lesbian and gay', as Stephen Angelides (1994:68) discovered:

> A cursory scan of the pages of two of Australia's lesbian and gay newspapers—*Melbourne Star Observer* and *Sydney Star Observer*—highlights the extent to which the term queer is being deployed in this context. From 'Queer Cartoons' to queer film to letters to the editor section entitled 'Queerly Speaking', the pages are saturated with queer references directed specifically at the lesbian and gay community.

Recent books similarly favour queer in titles such as *Queering the Pitch: The New Lesbian and Gay Musicology* (Brett et al., 1994) and *A Queer Romance: Lesbians, Gay Men and Popular Culture*

(Burston and Richardson, 1995). At other times, queer is deployed to indicate a critical distance from the identity politics that under-pin traditional notions of lesbian and gay community. In this sense, queer marks a suspension of identity as something fixed, coherent and natural. But queer may also be used to signify a dif-ferent kind of identity which is consistent and self-identical, as in the case of some of the mobilisations of Queer Nation (see Chapter 8). Eschewing post-structuralist critiques of identity cate-gories, queer functions here more as a fashionable than a theor-etical term. It is used as a way of distinguishing old-style lesbians and gays from the new, where that distinction may be registered not so much historically as variations in the understanding of iden-tity formation but stylistically in, for example, body piercing. Or queer may be used to describe an open-ended constituency, whose shared characteristic is not identity itself but an anti-normative positioning with regard to sexuality. In this way, queer may exclude lesbians and gay men whose identification with com-munity and identity marks a relatively recent legitimacy, but include all those whose sexual identifications are not considered normal or sanctioned.

Like the theory of performativity, which to a large extent under-writes its project, queer opts for denaturalisation as its primary strategy. It demarcates 'a domain virtually synonymous with homosexuality and yet wonderfully suggestive of a whole range of sexual possibilities . . . that challenge the familiar distinction between normal and pathological, straight and gay, masculine men and feminine women' (Hanson, 1993:138). Like early gay lib-erationism, queer confounds the categories that license sexual normativity; it differs from its predecessor by avoiding the delu-sion that its project is to uncover or invent some free, natural and primordial sexuality. By rejecting what Michael Warner (1993a: xxvi) calls the 'minoritizing logic of toleration or simple political interest-representation', and favouring instead 'a more thorough resistance to regimes of the normal', it demonstrates its under-standing that sexuality is a discursive effect. Since queer does not assume for itself any specific materiality or positivity, its resistance to what it differs from is necessarily relational rather than oppositional.

Queer has tended to occupy a predominantly sexual register. Recent signs indicate, however, that its denaturalising project is being brought to bear on other axes of identification than sex and gender. Describing queer as both 'anti-assimilationist and anti-separatist', Rosemary Hennessy (1994:86–7) argues that the queer project marks 'an effort to speak from and to the differences and silences that have been suppressed by the homo–hetero binary, an effort to unpack the monolithic identities "lesbian" and "gay", including the intricate ways lesbian and gay sexualities are inflected by heterosexuality, race, gender, and ethnicity'. Sedgwick (1993a:9) makes an even stronger claim when she observes that, in recent work, queer is being spun outward

> along dimensions that can't be subsumed under gender and sexuality at all: the ways that race, ethnicity, postcolonial nationality criss-cross with these *and other* identity-constituting, identity-fracturing discourses, for example. Intellectuals and artists of color whose sexual self-definition includes 'queer' . . . are using the leverage of 'queer' to do a new kind of justice to the fractal intricacies of language, skin, migration, state.

Although some complain that queer encodes a Eurocentric bias, which makes it insensitive to the largely identity-based politics of ethnic communities (Maggenti, 1991; Malinowitz, 1993), the recent work that Sedgwick here refers to indicates that queer's denaturalising impulse may well find an articulation within precisely those contexts to which it has been judged indifferent.

Clearly, there is no generally acceptable definition of queer; indeed, many of the common understandings of the term contradict each other irresolvably. Nevertheless, the inflection of queer that has proved most disruptive to received understandings of identity, community and politics is the one that problematises normative consolidations of sex, gender and sexuality—and that, consequently, is critical of all those versions of identity, community and politics that are believed to evolve 'naturally' from such consolidations. By refusing to crystallise in any specific form, queer maintains a relation of resistance to whatever constitutes the normal. While bearing in mind the multiple and even contradictory sites signified by queer, *Queer Theory* emphasises this aspect of queer, and the analytical pressure it brings to bear on what Sedgwick (1993a:8) calls 'the open mesh of possibilities, gaps, overlaps, dissonances and resonances, lapses and excesses of meaning where the constituent elements of anyone's gender, of anyone's sexuality aren't made (or *can't* be made) to signify monolithically'.

Contestations of Queer

Although queer can be described as a logical development in twentieth-century gay and lesbian politics and scholarship, its progress has not been uncontentious. As the point of convergence for a potentially infinite number of non-normative subject positions, queer is markedly unlike those traditional political movements which ground themselves in a fixed and necessarily exclusionist identity. In stretching the boundaries of identity categories, and in seeming to disregard the distinctions between various forms of marginalised sexual identification, queer has provoked exuberance in some quarters, but anxiety and outrage in others. The various contestations of the term demonstrate the implications and investments of queer, clarifying its ambitions and limitations.

Queer scepticism about the self-evident status of identity categories has itself come under suspicion from those who think it is a merely apolitical or even reactionary form of intellectualising. In an extreme example of this, Susan J. Wolfe and Julia Penelope (1993:5) introduce their recent anthology of lesbian cultural criticism by identifying the destabilisation of identity as an explicitly homophobic strategy:

> We [cannot] afford to allow privileged patriarchal discourse (of which poststructuralism is but a new variant) to erase the collective identity Lesbians have only recently begun to establish ... For what has in fact resulted from the incorporation of

deconstructive discourse, in academic 'feminist' discourse at least, is that the word *Lesbian* has been placed in quotation marks, whether used or mentioned, and the existence of real Lesbians has been denied, once again.

Such objections to the interrogation of seemingly self-evident identity categories appeal almost generically to common sense. The stability and extra-discursive properties of lesbian identity are taken for granted by Wolfe and Penelope (ibid.:9) when they complain that what 'might have seemed a trivially obvious fact two decades ago, has been challenged by poststructuralist thought'. Less truculent is Bonnie Zimmerman's anxious observation that 'the discourses of "common sense" and contemporary theory seem to be moving further and further apart' (quoted in Palmer, 1993:6). Terry Castle (1993:13) expresses a similar disquiet when she critiques the way in which 'especially among younger lesbian and gay scholars trained in Continental philosophy (including a number of the so-called queer theorists) it has recently become popular to contest, along deconstructionist lines, the very meaningfulness of terms such as *lesbian* or *gay* or *coming out*'. Claiming on the contrary that 'we live in a world in which the word *lesbian* still makes sense, and that it is possible to use the word frequently, even lyrically, and still be understood', she takes the self-evidence of lesbian as the basis of her engaging and transhistorical study of that figure (ibid.:14). But in her critique of Castle, Valerie Traub (1995:99) argues that such claims ignore the ideological dimension of appeals to common sense:

> The assumption that one knows, in an 'ordinary', 'vernacular' sense, what a 'lesbian' is (*Apparitional Lesbian* 15), and that on the basis of such stable knowledge one can forge connections across time and culture, obscures the recognition that such knowledge is less a position from which one can make autonomous claims than the result of normalizing discourses.

Such reliance on what everybody already knows is rhetorically but not intellectually persuasive. For what is being critiqued in contemporary theory is the very notion of the natural, the obvious, and the taken-for-granted. 'The appeal to so-called "common

sense"', writes Lee Edelman (1994:xviii) 'reinforces the hypostati-
zation [reification] of the "natural" upon which homophobia relies
and thus partakes of an ideological labor complicit with heterosexual supremacy'. To valorise common sense is naive, if not dan-
gerous. For it does not follow that those formations of knowledge
which coincide with the discourses of common sense manifest
some truth beyond analysis. Rather, the convergence of knowledge and common sense may be understood more profitably as
licensing the operation of unexamined ideological structures.

Another common objection to the recent queering of lesbian
and gay identities focuses on political efficacy: to question the self-
evident status of identity (so the argument goes) may well be
explicable in intellectual terms but is indefensible because it
encourages apolitical quietism. In this evaluation, the assumption
that provides the rationale for identity politics in the first place—
namely, a coherent and unified identity is a prerequisite for effective political action—also structures the criticism of any suspension of identity. However, while the strenuous reworking of
traditional understandings of lesbian and gay has revalued what
might constitute effective political action, recent challenges to a
now recognisably 1970s style of identity politics do not discredit
the notion of politics itself. 'The deconstruction of identity is not
the deconstruction of politics', Butler (1990:148) points out:
'rather, it establishes as political the very terms through which
identity is articulated'.

Perhaps the simplest objection to queer comes from those one
might expect to be among its constituents, and yet are neither
interpellated by the term nor persuaded that the new category
describes or represents them. Often accounted for in terms of 'a
gay generation gap', this objection comes from those who cannot
accept a once pejorative term as a positive self-description (Reed,
1993). Much of this discussion is informal, even anecdotal. When
the Queer Studies List recently debated on the Internet the
assumption of a queer identity, some postings argued for its adoption, and others against. While some were happy to call themselves queer, and others refused to do so, one correspondent
testified to his ambivalence about this nomenclature: 'Every time I
hear "that" word, I want to feel empowered and use it myself.

Instead, my feelings get hurt. I adolesced [sic] in the late 60's early 70's as well. I'll get over it. My younger gay friends are now using faggot. Ugh!' (D'Arc, 1995). In canvassing various responses to queer, Stephen Jones (1992:26) is similarly anxious about the perceived attractiveness of the new terminology: 'In my need to be considered a contemporary gay man I've felt increasingly pressured for the last two years to describe myself as a queer. I do so self-consciously, not confident that we yet have a common understanding of queer politics and culture'. The reluctance of certain gay men and lesbians to identify themselves unequivocally as queer demonstrates that the categories are not synonymous. As Sedgwick (1993b:13) observes 'there are some lesbians and gays who could never count as queer, and other people who vibrate to the chord of queer without having much same-sex eroticism, or without routing their same-sex eroticism through the identity labels lesbian or gay'.

Those who adopt or reject queer as a self-identifying term are often opposed in their conception of its political usefulness. Proponents of the new terminology argue that to redeploy the term queer as a figure of pride is a powerful act of cultural reclamation, and strategically useful in removing the word from that homophobic context in which it formerly flourished. Citing as their precedent the transvaluation of 'dyke' from a term of abuse to an assertive and then routinely casual declaration of lesbian identity, advocates of queer argue that changes of nomenclature can influence or even transform cultural assumptions and knowledges. Opponents of the new terminology, however, point out that merely to change the semantic value of queer is to misrecognise a symptom for the disease. They argue that even if its resignification were to prove successful, other words or neologisms would take on the cultural work it once did. After all, the successful neutralisation of the term dyke has not resulted in the end of discrimination against lesbians.

There is some merit in each of these arguments. Whatever social transformations may be secured by proliferating queer as a positive term of self-description, they will be neither absolute nor uncontestable. Even though queer has been appropriated by a new generation, which recognises itself in that term without equivocation, homophobia is not going to be rendered speechless or lack an intelligible vocabulary with which to make itself understood. Yet neither is the semantic struggle over queer useless despite the fact that some critics like Julia Parnaby (1993:14) think that the resignification of queer is an empty, because purely linguistic, gesture:

> Reclaiming 'Queer' as a name is based on the assumption that merely to do so strips it of its homophobic power, that it turns the world against the queer basher, rather than the bashed. It is a direct consequence of post-structuralist arguments around language which claim that the meanings of words are constantly redefined each time they are used by the individuals who use them, and that we can therefore make words mean what we want them to mean.

Parnaby devalues queer because she assumes incorrectly that when post-structuralists describe the production of meaning as contingent (that is, dependent on its context) they mean that it is voluntarist (that is, determined by the individual subject of enunciation). Although words do not simply mean what we want them to mean, such labels are more than merely new descriptions for old realities. Because the word queer indexes—and to some extent constitutes—changed models of gender and sexuality, semantic struggles over its deployment are far from pointless.

There is also concern that the pejorative sense of queer will survive attempts at political reclamation. This seems likely given that much of its appeal derives from the way it resists even that limited legitimation achieved by the terms lesbian and gay. If queer is ever neutralised as a purely descriptive term, the denaturalising cultural work it currently undertakes will become ineffectual. The always derogatory underbelly of queer may well be one of its most valuable characteristics, according to Sedgwick (1993a:4):

> The main reason why the self-application of 'queer' by activists has proved so volatile is that there's no *way* that any amount of affirmative reclamation is going to succeed in detaching the word from its associations with shame and with the terrifying powerlessness of gender-dissonant or otherwise stigmatized

childhood. If queer is a politically potent term, which it is, that's because, far from being capable of being detached from the childhood source of shame, it cleaves to that scene as a near inexhaustible source of transformational energy.

Given the extent to which queer signifies a 'resistance to regimes of the normal', its immunity to domestication guarantees its capacity to maintain a critical relation to standards of normativity (Warner, 1993a:xxvi).

Anxiety that 'queer' will continue to connote perversion and illegitimacy has led some to argue that its adoption is politically a counter-productive gesture. 'Its use only serves to fuel existing prejudice', writes Simon Watney (1992:18), 'and may even lead to an increase in discrimination and violence'. The objection is that, in choosing to resignify a word which until recently circulated in the coarse register of slang, advocates of queer alienate themselves and their cause from people sympathetic to lesbian and gay grievances and inequities. Campion Reed thinks that to promote queer as a descriptive term may 'only give greater license to heterosexuals to employ degrading language', and cannot imagine politicians discussing '"queers" and "faggots" on the senate floor' (quoted in Angelides, 1994:83). Those who seek to effect political transformation under the rubric of queer have little patience for this line of argument, since they understand that, as long as political intervention is constrained by the very system it opposes, political success will necessarily be limited. The kind of legitimation achieved by lesbians and gays, they argue, is not to be emulated for it is evidence that they have sold out and betrayed their radical origins in gay liberation. Those lesbians and gays who are committed to achieving social change by means of democratically sanctioned structures allege that the queer position is too politically naive and idealistic to be effective. Ignorant of the real machineries of power, queers will not be able to achieve anything from the marginalised position they champion.

Proponents of each side of this argument are critical of both the other's politics and the limitations of the other side's political strategy. Those organising around queer principles foresee that any progress made by lesbians and gays will always be curtailed by their acquiescence to the larger system. Lesbians and gays, on the other hand, anticipate that queer demands will neither be listened to nor acted upon, since they are not channelled through the legitimate institutions of power. Despite their differences, both the lesbian and gay and the queer arguments understand politics in the same way, in so far as both sides imagine that the politics of certain strategies are self-evident before they are put into practice. This is a fairly common assumption, and not unique to these two groups. Nevertheless—and not least because it is held so widely and uncritically—this understanding of politics requires consideration. For as Diana Fuss (1989:105) argues, 'politics . . . represents the aporia in much of our current political theorizing', and 'that which signifies activism is least actively interrogated'. Instead of thinking of politics as the essential quality—known and evaluated in advance—of any given intervention, it is perhaps more proper to think of it as that which comes into being as the consequence not only of a specific strategy but also of the contexts with which that strategy meshes, if not randomly, then in unforeseen ways. Politics, then, may be understood helpfully as 'a set of effects and not a first cause or final determinant' (Fuss, 1989:106). Queer is sensitive to this open-ended construction of politics, since it represents itself as unfixed, and as holding open a space whose potential can never be known in the present.

The high profile of American activist groups working under the banner of Queer Nation in the early 1990s has drawn critical attention to the claims of queer nationalism. Documenting the origins and aims of Queer Nation, Alexander Chee (1991:15) notes its rapid ascendency: begun in April 1990, it was on 'the front page of the *Village Voice* by midsummer', and had gone from 'anonymity to scandal to celebrity within weeks'. Although most mobilisations of queer have not relied on the concept of nation, Queer Nation has been credited with popularising queer in America by giving 'the signifier "queer" national publicity' (Hennessy, 1994:86). It might be credited also with Americanising the term in other national contexts, in so far as David Phillips (1994:16) observes that 'a somewhat cynical reading of the profile of "queer" in Australia might argue that its usage is yet another instance of reflex mimicry of the United States of America'. Nationalism has long been an organising trope in the historical development of lesbian and gay politics, as is evident in such diverse mainfestations as Hirschfeld's 'third sex', the separatist Lesbian Nation, and the ethnic model of lesbian and gay identity (Duggan, 1992:16). Formed at an ACT UP meeting held in New York in 1990, Queer Nation 'began . . . without a name or a charter or a statement of purpose' (Chee, 1991:15). Calls to nationalism, however, tend to embody troublesome ideas of homogeneity and cohesion. In this respect, Queer Nation strikes David Phillips (1994:17) as being an oxymoronic formulation, since it 'conflates an ethnic model of origins and difference with a body of theoretical work which seeks to dismantle potentially essentialist models of identity' (cf. Zimmerman, 1995).

David Halperin (1995:63) reinforces this assessment of Queer Nation when he describes it as less queer than ACT UP, appropriating many of the latter's strategies only to create 'a movement of young lesbian and gay radicals defined by no other issue than that of sexual orientation'. Similarly, Lisa Duggan (1992:21) contends that 'Queer Nation, for some, is quite simply a gay nationalist organization'. Yet some argue that, by juxtaposing queerness with nationality, Queer Nation successfully denaturalises conservative and essentialist understandings of nationhood (Brasell, 1995). Consequently, it produces 'multiple and ambiguous' concepts of nation, which 'simulate "the national" with a camp inflection', and 'capitalize on the difficulty of locating the national public, whose consent to self-expression founds modern national identity' (Berlant and Freeman, 1992:152, 151). Although queered understandings of the national have the potential to refigure the nation as 'a newly defined political entity, better able to cross boundaries and construct more fluid identities', Queer Nation is often critiqued for drawing on less progressive formulations of nationality (Duggan, 1992:21). In their lengthy and largely sympathetic analysis of queer nationality, Berlant and Freeman (1992:170) conclude that Queer Nation's 'campaign has not yet . . . left behind the fantasies of glamour and homogeneity that characterize American nationalism itself'. Henry Abelove (1993:26) identifies this conflation of queer and American nationalisms when, after discussing his involvement in the Salt Lake City chapter of Queer Nation, he disarmingly concludes: 'And what of the name Queer Nation? I do not think that the signification of this name is as mysterious and difficult as most commentators on the subject have assumed. What Queer Nation really means is America'. Berlant and Freeman (ibid.:171) argue that Queer Nation fails to disarticulate its inflection of nationalism from a more recognisable version of Americanness: 'insofar as it assumes that "Queer" is the only insurgent "foreign" identity its citizens have, Queer Nation remains bound to the genericizing logic of American citizenship and to the horizon of an official formalism—one that equates sexual object choice with individual self-identity'. This reinstallation of queer identity— as something fixed, stable and known—within the template of national identity does not fulfil the radically denaturalising potential of queer.

While the success of queer is often measured in terms of its widespread acceptance, this has equally been a source of anxiety for some. The alacrity with which queer has caught on has been widely criticised, especially by those who think that in terms of style rather than substance it has produced 'a version of identity politics as postmodern commodity fetishism' (Edelman, 1994:114). Such vogueishness, complains Donald Morton (1993b:151), 'trivializes the very notion of queerness by reducing it to nothing more than a "lifestyle", certain ways of talking, walking, eating, dressing, having your hair cut and having sex'. The queering of the academy has been an equally swift process. Michael Warner (1992:18) notes: 'Academics now are talking about queer theory as a Movement. As recently as two years ago, the phrase would not have rung a bell'.

There is a suspicion that if queer can be institutionalised so readily and swiftly, it cannot sustain a radical critique. According to Donald Morton (1993a:123), 'the "dreamlike" success of Queer Theory today is enabled precisely by its tendency to endorse and celebrate the dominant academy's narrative of progressive change'. Rosemary Hennessy (1994:105) argues that, in conditions of late capitalism, queer is being appropriated in order to consolidate a hegemonic postmodern culture: 'Challenges to naturalized notions of identity and difference emanating from Madison Avenue and Wall Street', she writes, 'share a certain ideological affiliation with avant-garde queer theory'. Moreover, while queer's rapid expansion in the academy can be explained largely in terms of an older and more slowly established model of lesbian and gay studies, queer theory is often represented as having a greater investment in the institutional than in the political. The professionalisation of queer has mostly benefited those relatively few individuals who are making academic careers as queer scholars (Malinowitz, 1993:172). This suspicion is often registered in disquiet about queer theory's increasingly specialised vocabulary and analytical models, both of which are taken as evidence that queer theorists are not accountable to any community outside the universities. 'Right now', Malinowitz (ibid.) complains,

> overrepresented by prestigious academic institutions, drawing on closed-circuit calls for papers, using a post-structuralist vocabulary that unabridged dictionaries haven't yet caught up with, heavily interreferential and overwhelmingly white, the queer theorist network often resembles a social club open only to residents of a neighbourhood most of us can't afford to live in.

Reviewing a couple of recent theoretical works, Sherri Paris (1993:988) makes the standard criticism that queer theory is elitist and inaccessible: 'This is a politics formulated from a point beyond the body by people who are not hungry or cold, people who can theorize in comfort, peering at the world through computer screens, reconfiguring its surfaces endlessly, like a floppy disc'. Paris rehearses a familar characterisation of intellectuals, whose privilege is said to insulate them from the 'reality' they nevertheless feel licensed to analyse. However, her criticism also raises issues which have become particularly contentious within queer theory, where the continuities and discontinuities of theory and politics, individual and community, specialisation and accountability, are all debated.

In an essay which values the developments of queer theory but wants post-Stonewall theorising to be more in touch with its communities, Jeffrey Escoffier assesses the development of lesbian and gay studies in America. He finds that whereas they first developed out of (or even in tandem with) grass-roots political action, the 'successful institutionalization of lesbian and gay studies within the university' has given rise to a new generation of scholars, whose interests are textual rather than social, and who are 'primarily concerned with building up the intellectual status of the field' (Escoffier, 1990:41, 47). If queer theory is to avoid becoming 'unrepresentative and intellectually narrow', he argues (ibid.:48), 'lesbian and gay studies must remain in dialogue with the communities that gave rise to the political and social conditions for its existence'. It should be noted, however, that queer theory does not simply default on the commitment of lesbian and gay studies to politics and community; what it does is call into question the knowledges which maintain such concepts as if they were self-evident and indisputable. When Escoffier (ibid.:40) writes that 'the growth of gay and lesbian studies forces an examination of whether as an academic discipline it should, or can, exist without structural ties to lesbian and gay political struggles', he relies on a distinction between theory and politics that many queer theorists are intent on problematising.

For the notion that there is a lesbian and gay community—definable in so far as it is distinct from those academics whose accountability is being solicited—is one that queer theory questions. Furthermore, it is not simply a question of where that community might be located—on the streets, if the anti-intellectual rhetoric is to be trusted—but of how its interventions come to be 'political' in ways that are denied academic work. For according to Foucault's account of how power and resistance work across multiplicitous networks to unchoreographed effect, it is far from clear that writing a paper, or developing an analytical framework, is any less effective than various other gestures, long recognised in lesbian and gay circles as unambiguously political, such as setting up pickets, writing to government representatives and organising rallies and marches. Moreover, even if queer theorists felt obliged to represent the concerns of a specific community, the expectation that queer theory would be intelligible to a varied and non-specialist readership would limit the extent of the denaturalising work it might undertake (Edelman, 1994:xvi–xviii).

Perhaps the most controversial deployment of queer is as an umbrella term for dissimilar subjects, whose collectivity is underwritten by a mutual engagement in non-normative sexual practices or identities.[1] In its broadest usages, queer describes not only lesbian and gay, but also—and not exhaustively—transsexual, transgender and bisexual individuals. As what Louise Sloan calls 'the oxymoronic community of difference' (quoted in Duggan, 1992:19), queer posits a commonality between people which does not disallow their fundamental difference. Yet the ubiquity of queer raises the possibility that the term will either be taken over by a liberal pluralism notorious for its 'capacity for cooption and depoliticization' (Grosz, 1995:249) or erased by 'the ancient and persistent specter of sexual despecification' (Halperin, 1995:65). Leo Bersani (1995:71, 73) raises both of these concerns when he describes queer as having a 'de-gaying' effect that is not so very different from the 'remarkably familiar, and merely liberal, version' of lesbian and gay despecification. While the open-endedness of queer has been much celebrated, the subsequent claim that it is a more radical formation than lesbian and gay has been critiqued. For instance, David Phillips (1994:16) protests that

> the inclusionist ambitions of queer—the attempt to represent not only gays and lesbians, transgenderists, and even heterosexuals as 'straight-identified queers', *et cetera*—has had the effect of not only effacing the specific political identities, needs and agendas of these various groups but that, in doing so, queer has produced a new closet as any specific self-identification as either gay or lesbian (predicated upon same-sex practices) is disavowed.

Queer's totalising gesture is seen as having the potential to work against lesbian and gay specificity, and to devalue those analyses of homophobia and heterocentrism developed largely by lesbian and gay critics.

Other anxieties generated by the potential unboundedness of queer are that it will neutralise the efficacy of lesbian and gay as an identificatory category, and that its flexibility will connect lesbians and gay men with others whose commitment to anti-homophobic politics is disputed. Although Elizabeth Grosz (1995: 249–50) concedes that part of queer's appeal is 'an ambiguity about what the term "queer" refers to', some of the things it might refer to make it a risky political category:

'Lesbian and Gay' has the advantage of straightforwardly articulating its constituency, while 'queer' is capable of accommodating, and will not [sic] doubt provide a political rationale and coverage in the near future for many of the most blatant and extreme forms of heterosexual and patriarchal power games. They too are, in a certain sense, queer, persecuted, ostracized. Heterosexual sadists, pederasts, fetishists, pornographers, pimps, voyeurs suffer from social sanctions: in a certain sense they too can be regarded as oppressed. But to claim an oppression of the order of lesbian and gay, women's or racial oppression is to ignore the very real complicity and phallic rewards of what might be called 'deviant sexualities' within patriarchal and heterocentric power relations.

Certainly the prospect of being politically mobilised in the interests of those whose sexual practices or identities are understood as antithetical to the broadly progressive politics traditionally articulated by lesbians and gay men is often identified as a major deficiency of the queer model. There is little agreement, however, on which groups politically compromise a lesbian and gay affinity with queer, although most commentators nominate paedophiles in that category. On the other hand, David Halperin (1995:62) writes that queer 'could include some married couple without children, for example, or even (who knows?) some married couples *with* children—with, perhaps, *very naughty* children'. Grosz.elsewhere singles out pederasts and bisexuals as groups which, in different ways, complicate lesbian and gay mobilisations of queer (Leng and Ross, 1994:7–8). Stephen Angelides (1994:78) identifies 'rape, paedophilia, and "snuff" sexual practices' as problematising queer, while Sheila Jeffreys (1993:146) specifies '"pedophilia" or "sadomasochism"'. These debates about what constitutes proper or ethical sexual behaviour are not new. After all, the boundaries drawn around identity-based lesbian and gay politics have been violently contested at various times in debates about sadomasochism, intergenerational sex and pornography. However, queer raises the possibility of locating sexual perversion as the very precondition of an identificatory category, rather than as a destabilisation or a variation of it. While this allows hypothetically for a collectivity comprising all forms of non-normative sexuality, the open-endedness of queer neither forces coalitional alliances nor rules out negotiations with the ethical. Despite Grosz's prediction (1995:249, 250) that queer will be hijacked in 'the near future' by an unruly band of heterosexual perverts committed to the maintenance of 'heterocentric power relations', the historical circumstances in which the term evolved have maintained its affiliation with anti-homophobic politics. While future developments of queer remain unknown, there is no sign of a change in the term's fundamental orientation. So, although the 'straight queer' phenomenon has been much criticised (Kamp, 1993), discussions by self-identified straight queers tend to be marked by an almost painful tentativeness and self-reflexivity, and couched in terms of anti-homophobic analysis (Powers, 1993).

In producing a coalition of non-normative sexual identities, queer has often been accused of working against the recent visibility and political gains of lesbians and gay men. The hard-won respectability and sense of community afforded by identifying oneself as lesbian or gay is lost in a term whose only specificity is its resistance to convention. Much criticism of queer as a self-description is predicated on a desire to maintain legitimacy: 'The last thing I want to do', writes Eric Marcus, 'is institutionalize that difference by defining myself with a word and a political philosophy that set me outside the mainstream' (quoted in Garber, 1995:65). This rejection of queer is most often the result of that sense of belonging made possible by the recent legitimation of 'gay' as both a term and a constituency. David Link (1993:47) confesses: 'I have wrestled with myself over whether, as a gay man, I am Queer. I have decided that I am not. *Queer* is the word of the Other, of the Outsider. I do not feel like I am outside anything due to my sexual orientation'. Similarly, in a letter to the editor of a Sydney lesbian and gay newspaper, Craig Johnston writes:

> Don't expect me, even after 20 years of gay/lesbian radicalism, to assume our struggle is no longer valid. And when I say 'our', I mean gay and lesbian . . . 'Queer' is anti-homosexual. The

'queer' community does not exist. Queer is the enemy. When I hear 'Queer' I reach for the Kalashnikov. (quoted in Galbraith, 1993:22)

The flip side to Johnston's antipathy to queer is that version of queer politics which devalues the categories of lesbian and gay by representing them as dated, elitist, establishment, and consolidated by a middle-class emphasis on commodity and capital; as Steven Cossen (1991:22) puts it, 'trying to purchase the right goods at Macy's to demonstrate they are just like everybody else except for what they wear to nightclubs'. A similar complaint is made by Jason Bishop when he says: 'I don't identify with the older generation of lesbian [sic] and gay men. Very cushy—brunch on Sunday and credit card shopping all week long' (quoted in ibid.:16).

Paradoxically, gay liberation's—albeit limited—success in securing legitimacy and improved conditions for gays and lesbians is identified in these complaints as the source of a queer dissatisfaction with the extent to which gays and lesbians have been complicit with a heterosexual power-structure fundamentally indifferent or inimical to them. Despite—or perhaps because of—the gains made by gay liberationist struggles and interventions, those committed to the more aggressive tactics of queer argue against the efficacy of democratically sanctioned channels of political intervention like organising rallies, lobbying and petitioning. Developments which seemed impossible as recently as thirty years ago—such as explicitly lesbian and gay businesses, government or local-body funding for lesbian and gay community groups, and the recognition that lesbian and gay constituencies can be targeted as an economic or electoral force—are seen by those committed to a queer agenda as signs not of progress but of how lesbians and gays have been assimilated into mainstream culture and values. There is no denying a certain mutual hostility between what becomes constituted by such antagonisms as two camps. Lesbians and gays are sometimes represented as being complacent, and part of the system—so much so that they dismiss queer as nothing more than an immature and generational rebellion against the parental authority of lesbian and gay categories (Fenster, 1993: 87–8). Others are afraid that queer might 'provide a ready-made instrument of homophobic disavowal', and thus enable 'trendy and glamorously unspecified sexual outlaws' to stigmatise and dismiss those still committed to 'an old-fashioned, essentialized, rigidly defined, specifically sexual (namely, *lesbian* or *gay*) identity' (Halperin, 1995:65).

Even more anxiety has been expressed about the possible erosion of lesbians in queer. For many lesbians, queer offers an antidote to the perceived limitations of lesbian feminism, which include its categorisation of lesbians as 'women' rather than 'homosexuals', and its at times prescriptive accounts of what ought to constitute the sexual (Smyth, 1992:36–46). While queer lays ambitious claim to gender neutrality, there is a well-founded suspicion that such claims more commonly conceal a generic masculinity. When Teresa de Lauretis first advocated the term queer in 1991, she charged it with the responsibility of countering the masculinist bias latent in that naturalised and seemingly gender-sensitive phrase, 'lesbian and gay'. The business of queer theory, she wrote at that time, was to remedy that 'continuing failure of representation' which had resulted in an 'enduring silence on the specificity of lesbianism in the contemporary "gay and lesbian" discourse' (de Lauretis, 1991:vi–vii). Just as feminists refused to accept the masculine pronoun as an ungendered universal term— sensing in the scholarly insistence on that grammatical 'rule' a more sinister ideological investment—so there is now some reluctance to allow the gender non-specificity of queer. There is an even more relevant precedent for this anxiety. 'Lesbian' itself began to circulate widely only when a nascent lesbian feminism became disillusioned with masculinist bias in the priorities of both the homophile and subsequently gay liberation movements. So, for many lesbian feminists, the rise of queer and its claims to gender non-specificity already evoke an unwelcome sense of *déjà vu*. Many of the arguments about the gendering of queer originate in lesbian feminist rather than gay liberationist concerns. While it would be a mistake to understand these two social movements as being opposed to—or even always clearly distinguishable from— one another, the lesbian feminist objections to queer are undoubtedly significant.

Philippa Bonwick (1993:10) makes what has become the standard lesbian feminist objection to queer when she writes: 'Perhaps the most damaging aspect of the pervasive push to be queer is that it shrouds lesbians in an ever thicker cloak of invisibility . . . Queer totally ignores the politics of gender. Using a generic term wipes out women again'. Bonwick here reiterates a common concern that queer politics will be insensitive to differences of gender within that allegedly inclusive category. Noting queer's 'universalising aspirations', Terry Castle (1993:12) attributes its recent popularity to the way in which 'it makes it easy to enfold female homosexuality back "into" male homosexuality and disembody the lesbian once again'. Sheila Jeffreys (1994:460) detects in queer a gay male agenda 'inimical to women's and lesbian interests'. Given that she finds gay men at the very heart of male supremacy, it is perhaps not surprising that she represents queer as an insidious attempt to reinstall lesbians in a structure of inequity in relation to gay men: 'Another way in which lesbians are being pulled back into cultural subordination to gay men is through "queer" politics' (Jeffreys, 1993: 143). Having described lesbian feminism as breaking away from the masculinist concerns of gay liberation, Jeffreys figures queer as a backlash phenomenon: what masquerades as a new descriptive model is merely an old one cunningly operating under a new name.

Julia Parnaby also sees queer as a movement committed to furthering a masculinist agenda at the expense of those lesbians who misrecognise themselves as incorporated into that category: 'By falsely assuming that lesbians and gay men have shared interests', she writes, 'Queer aims to provide an arena where men and women work together to fight men's battles' (Parnaby, 1993:14). Arguing that 'as long as [queer] continues to be a male-led movement there will never be any serious considerations of issues relating specifically to women', Parnaby adds in a footnote: 'Hence the emphasis on AIDS for example; whilst breast cancer, which is reaching enormous proportions amongst lesbians is never mentioned' (ibid.:16). This suggestion that lesbians have organised under the rubric of 'queer' within the framework of the AIDS epidemic whereas gay men remain indifferent to issues of lesbian health—here breast but elsewhere cervical cancer—is reasonably common in such criticism. No one would be interested in imagining a lesbian-inflected version of the AIDS epidemic in order to test the hypothesis that, in this instance, gay men would not reciprocate the support and efforts of lesbians in the AIDS crisis. However, it is worth observing that AIDS and breast (or cervical) cancer are not at present discursively equivalent. Whereas AIDS is frequently read as a metonym for homosexuality, breast and/or cervical cancer are more commonly understood as an index of not specifically lesbian but women's health. The 'truth' of these rhetorical constructions might be contested productively. Nevertheless, while lesbians remain largely unaffected epidemiologically by AIDS, its discursive struggles interpellate them as homosexuals far more comprehensively than gay men would ever be implicated in a comparable health crisis instigated by breast or cervical cancer. Although Thomas Yingling (1991:293) also considers 'the oft-repeated assertion that, were the gay medical crisis of the 80s a woman's health crisis gay men would not be working for the cause with the fervor or numbers with which lesbians have responded to the crisis of AIDS', he identifies as significant the visibility of gender as opposed to sexual difference, and the 'complex and equivocal' symbolic work effected by 'white gay male culture'. Moreover, the discursive frameworks which constitute AIDS and breast or cervical cancer are far from fixed, and it may well be activist strategies that refigure them. 'The AIDS activist movement . . . owes much to the women's health movement of the 70s', writes Sedgwick (1993a:15), 'and in another turn, an activist politics of breast cancer, spearheaded by lesbians, seems in the last year or two to have been emerging based on the models of AIDS activism'.

Cherry Smyth (1992:35), herself an enthusiastic advocate of queer, has reservations about queer's gender politics:

> While queer raises the possibility of dealing with complex subjectivities and differences in terms of gender, race and class, it also risks not trying hard enough to resist the reductive prescriptiveness some of us suffered in feminism and the uncritical essentialism that privileges the queerness of gay white men. While it offers lesbians an escape from unilateral lesbian orthodoxy into a more pluralistic and flexible politics, there is a dan-

ger of losing sight of the progressive aspects of feminism, which gave many of us the courage to speak.

In an article entitled 'Women as Queer Nationals', Maria Maggenti (1991:20) writes of her disillusionment with working under the masculinist rubric of queer:

> The map of the new queer nation would have a male face and . . . mine and those of my many colored sisters would simply be background material. We would be the demographic cosmetics, as it were, to assuage and complement the deeply imbedded prejudices and unselfconscious omissions of so many urgent and angry young men.

Theorists who are variously enthusiastic, ambivalent and hostile about the ramifications of queer as an identificatory category unanimously critique its tendency to disregard the specificities of gender. While the elimination of lesbians from a category that claims to represent them is wholly unacceptable, it is helpful to consider the relationship between feminism and queer in order to determine what status gender might have within a queer politics.

The field of queer-inflected lesbian and gay studies has been described as 'feminism-free' (Jeffreys, 1994:459). While '"queer theory" still seems . . . to denote primarily the study of male homosexuality' (Castle, 1993:13), it is more difficult to sustain a representation of queer as actively not feminist. For one thing many of the most prominent theorists in the area are undoubtedly feminist: Judith Butler, Douglas Crimp, Teresa de Lauretis, Jonathan Dollimore, Diana Fuss, Jonathan Goldberg, David Halperin, Mandy Merck, Eve Kosofsky Sedgwick, Valerie Traub and Jeffrey Weeks. It would be impossible to come up with a comparable list of equally well-known queer theorists whose work is *not* feminist. Furthermore, as an interdisciplinary formation, queer studies developed out of—and continues to be understandable in terms of—feminist knowledges. In describing *Between Men* (first published in 1985)—that monograph which is often, if hyperbolically, described as the point of origin for queer studies—Sedgwick (1992:viii) explains that she 'intended [it] very pointedly as a complicating, antiseparatist, and antihomophobic contribution to a feminist movement'.

Exactly how queer relates to gender can be understood by considering the recent and influential assertion that gender and sexuality—like feminist and anti-homophobic enquiry—are not the same thing. It follows from this distinction that the gender-based knowledges of feminism may not necessarily account for the entire field of human sexuality. These claims have been substantiated comprehensively by Sedgwick and Gayle Rubin, whose writings would be impossible to understand without the explanatory framework of feminism.

In her influential essay 'Thinking Sex' (1993), Rubin analyses the social construction of sex hierarchies and the consequent demonising of non-normative sexualities. She concludes that 'gender affects the operation of the sexual system, and the sexual system has had gender-specific manifestations. But although sex and gender are related, they are not the same thing, and they form the basis of two distinct arenas of social practice' (Rubin, 1993:33). While acknowledging the strengths of feminist analysis, Rubin argues (ibid.:34) that to expect feminism to theorise sexuality is to disadvantage both:

> Feminist conceptual tools were developed to detect and analyze gender-based hierarchies. To the extent that these overlap with erotic stratifications, feminist theory has some explanatory power. But as issues become less those of gender and more those of sexuality, feminist analysis becomes misleading and often irrelevant. Feminist thought simply lacks angles of vision which can fully encompass the social organization of sexuality.

Like Rubin, Sedgwick (1990:32) claims that

> it seems predictable that the analytic bite of a purely gender-based account will grow less incisive and direct as the distance of its subject from a social interface between different genders increases. It is unrealistic to expect a close, textured analysis of same-sex relations through an optic calibrated in the first place to the coarser stigmata of gender difference.

Criticising feminism's tendency to understand sexuality as 'a derivation of gender', Rubin (1993.:33, 34) calls for the development of 'an autonomous theory and politics specific to sexuality'.

Imagining a mutually productive relation between the theorising of gender and the theorising of sex, she asserts that 'feminism's critique of gender hierarchy must be incorporated into a radical theory of sex, and the critique of sexual oppression should enrich feminism' (ibid.:34).

Sedgwick draws on Rubin's call for a specific theorising of sexuality in formulating a framework for analysing twentieth-century understandings of homosexuality. Despite Sedgwick's reliance on Rubin's formulations, Butler (1994:8) points out that Rubin's 'call was not for a lesbian/gay theoretical frame, but for an analysis that might account for the regulation of a wide range of sexual minorities'. Consequently, Butler argues that 'the expansive and coalitional sense of "sexual minorities" cannot be rendered interchangeable with "lesbian and gay", and it remains an open question whether "queer" can achieve these same goals of exclusiveness' (ibid.:11). According to Sedgwick (1990:30) 'there is always at least the potential for an analytic distance between gender and sexuality' (1990:30). Although, like Rubin, she allows that sexuality and gender are thoroughly enmeshed with each other, she thinks that this is a historically specific consequence of the ways in which homosexuality and heterosexuality—rather than, say, certain sexual acts or relations of power—have come to define the field of sexuality, and therefore should not be allowed to shape the models of analysis:

> The definitional narrowing-down in this century of sexuality as a whole to a binarized calculus of *homo-* or *hetero*sexuality is a weighty fact but an entirely historical one. To use that fait accompli as a reason for conflating sexuality with gender would obscure the degree to which the fact itself requires explanation. (ibid.:31, original emphasis).

Moreover, Sedgwick argues that a reliance on gender-inflected analytical models may inadvertently mobilise heterosexist assumptions about the primacy of relations between genders. 'The ultimate definitional appeal in any gender-based analysis must necessarily be to the diacritical frontier between different genders', she writes (ibid.). 'This gives heterosocial and heterosexual relations a conceptual privilege of incalculable consequence.'

Although both Rubin and Sedgwick maintain that any theory of sexuality must be attentive to feminist analysis, Jeffreys (1994:466) sees them as further undermining lesbian and feminist principles: 'Another aspect of the new lesbian and gay studies that does not bode well for the interests of lesbians and feminists is the determination to establish that the study of sexuality is a field of inquiry quite separate from and *impervious to* feminist theory' (my emphasis). Jeffreys insists that an imperative to separate the analytical axis of sex from that of gender amounts to an indifference and imperviousness to feminism. Yet this is not evident in the work of those she thus tries to discredit. It is clear, for instance, that in making this argument Sedgwick continues to value and champion the very feminism which Jeffreys implies she betrays. One need only cite Sedgwick in order to demonstrate that the finely worked and qualified character of her proposition differs markedly from Jeffreys's paraphrase of it:

> This book will hypothesize, with Rubin, that the question of gender and the question of sexuality, *inextricable from one another though they are in that each can be expressed only in the terms of the other*, are nonetheless not the same question, that in twentieth-century Western culture gender and sexuality represent two analytical axes that may productively be imagined as being as distinct from one another as, say, gender and class, or class and race. Distinct, that is to say, *no more than minimally*, but nonetheless usefully. (Sedgwick, 1990:29, my emphasis)

This call to treat gender and sexuality as distinct but 'inextricable' categories does not establish 'the study of sexuality [as] a field of inquiry quite separate from and impervious to feminist theory'. But the insistence that gender and sexuality are not the same thing has often been taken to license 'a methodological distinction . . . which would distinguish theories of sexuality from theories of gender and, further, allocate the theoretical investigation of sexuality to queer studies, and the analysis of gender to feminism' (Butler, 1994:1). This neat allocation is often the inaugural gesture of a queer studies establishing its disciplinary boundaries. It is critiqued by Butler, who finds that the reduction of feminist interests to gender ignores significant aspects of recent feminist work. A narrow focus on gender cannot account for radical feminist work on sexual politics, race or class. Nor can it explain such feminist work as Butler's own, which seeks to complicate gender through sexuality (ibid.:15–16).

The distinction between gender and sexuality which under-writes the queer project is not in itself inimical to feminism. Never-theless, there are problems in formulating queer so persistently as a reaction against the allegedly anachronistic gender-based concerns of feminism. Biddy Martin (1994b:104) understands that the queer examinations of feminism are mutually productive, but is still 'worried about the occasions when antifoundational celebrations of queerness rely on their own projections of fixity, constraint, or subjection onto a fixed ground, often onto feminism or the female body, in relation to which queer sexualities become figural, performative, playful, and fun'. Martin expresses concern that queer theory frames feminism as a simplistic figure of opposition. In 'proceed[ing] . . . by way of polemical and ultimately reductionist accounts of the varieties of feminist approaches', it ends up with 'just one feminism, guilty of the humanist trap of making a self-same, universal category of "women"—defined as other than men—the subject of feminism' (ibid.:105). More significantly, this move associates women—and, as a corollary, feminism—with gender, and men with sexuality. Because such a model 'at least implicitly conceives gender in negative terms, in the terms of fixity, miring, or subjection to the indicatively female body', it follows 'that escape from gender, usually in the form of disembodiment and always in the form of gender crossings, becomes the goal and the putative achievement' (ibid.).[2]

Martin does not object on ethical or even political grounds to the identificatory practices or cultural forms of gender crossings that produce, say, the butch lesbian or the lesbian tomboy. What she questions is their seemingly self-evident claims to transgression. She points out that to theorise such gender crossings as deconstructive inadvertently establishes femininity or the lesbian femme as quietist, if not reactionary. While she wants to maintain the advantages of treating gender and sexuality as distinct but inextricable from one another, she argues that this will not simplify gender but instead multiply its 'permutations . . . with sexual aims, objects and practices'; as a result, 'identifications and desires that cross traditional boundaries' will not efface 'the complexities of gender identities and expressions' (ibid.:108). Butler similarly (1993b:28) emphasises the distinctive but dynamically interactive character of gender and sexuality when she writes: 'surely it is as unacceptable to insist that relations of sexual subordination determine gender position as it is to separate radically forms of sexuality from the workings of gender norms'. And Rosemary Hennessy (1994:106) thinks that

> if the point of queer critique is to develop critical frameworks that can disrupt and rewrite the countless ways the human potential for sensual pleasure is socially produced as sex, then we need a mode of analysis that can address the historicity of pleasure in all of its complexity, including its relation to gender.

In refusing to figure gender as relatively fixed or fundamental in comparison to the fluidity of sexuality's cross-identifications, Martin (1994b:117) opens up a space in which forms of femininity can be theorised productively:

> The three-dimensionality lent to gender by the complicated figure-ground relations among femmeness, femininity, and female anatomy exposes the fallacy of conceiving feminine identifications in passive terms, in terms of conformity, or comfort with the female body. Femmeness is as active a structuring of organism-psyche-social relations as apparently more defiant identities, or perhaps it would be more accurate to say that femmeness is an effect of as active a structuring as butchness is, that it involves a range of crossings and surprising routings and always assumes specific forms.

Martin advocates a *rapprochement* between feminist and queer theory. She urges that 'we stop defining queerness as mobile and fluid in relation to what then gets construed as stagnant and ensnaring, and as associated with a maternal, anachronistic, and putatively puritanical feminism'. She also advocates that we no longer 'see queer theory and activism as disruptive of the potential solidarities and shared interests among women' (Martin, 1994a:101). In focusing on feminine identifications, she negotiates

between feminist and queer models of gender and sexuality, identifying valuable and oversimplified elements in both.

The much commented upon burgeoning of queer is matched
by various contestations of its ascendancy. The struggle over
which terminology to use as the basis of political intervention
may well be the least productive effect of the recent rise of queer.
As David Halperin (1995:63) complains:

> the endless and fruitless debates among lesbians and gay men
> over the respective merits of 'gay' or 'lesbian' versus 'queer'
> have not only wasted a lot of energy and generated a lot of ill
> feeling but, more important, have inhibited careful evaluation
> of the strategic functioning of those terms, as if there could be
> any safety or security in adhering single-mindedly to the 'right'
> one (whichever one that might be).

Halperin argues that to structure the relation between 'lesbian' or
'gay' and 'queer' in terms of competition minimises queer's most
enabling intervention: its foregrounding of the strategic form and
precise use of any given terminological deployment.

By emphasising the pragmatic efficacy of identity categories
(rather than the supremacy of one particular terminology) it
becomes evident that queer in no way necessitates what gay
liberation once optimistically imagined as 'the end of the homosexual' (Altman, 1972:216). Neither the consolidations of the lesbian and gay movements nor even the continuing mobilisation of
'lesbian' and 'gay' as politicised descriptors challenge the queer
model. Disillusioned with traditional identity-based forms of political organisation and engaged in a radical denaturalisation of all
identity categories, queer operates not so much as an alternative
nomenclature—which would measure its success by the extent to
which it supplanted the former classifications of lesbian and gay—
than as a means of drawing attention to those fictions of identity
that stabilise all identificatory categories. While criticisms of queer
are often based on anxiety about the loss of lesbian and gay specificity, it is far from certain that this is the logical outcome of the
queer project.

The queer agenda is indeed marked by a refusal to naturalise
the interworkings of gender and desire to the extent that the

categories 'lesbian' and 'gay' do. But this is not to say that queer is committed to the extinction of those marginalised groups. As Simon Watney (1992:22) has observed:

> It is clear that not all gay men and lesbians will come to accept the term 'queer' in relation to themselves, even if they fully understand why other people find it useful. This is entirely for the good, since it serves to acknowledge that there are no natural or inevitable connexions uniting everyone whose identity is formed on the basis of homosexual object choice.

Queer has little to gain from establishing itself as a monolithic descriptive category. Consequently, queer and lesbian may well be two strategic identifications held simultaneously:

> Queer activists are also lesbians and gays in other contexts—as for example where leverage can be gained through bourgeois propriety, or through minority-rights discourse, or through more gender-marked language (it probably won't replace lesbian feminism). Queer politics has not just replaced older modes of lesbian and gay identity; it has come to exist alongside those older modes, opening up new possibilities and problems whose relation to more familiar problems is not always clear. (Warner, 1993b:xxvii)

Queer's impact on identity politics has yet to be determined. It is probable that identity politics will not disappear under the influence of queer but become more nuanced, less sure of itself, and more attuned to those multiple compromises and pragmatic effects that characterise *any* mobilisation of identity. Although frequently described as aggressive, queer is also tentative. Its suspicion of homogeneous identity categories and totalising explanatory narratives necessarily limits its own claims. It does not offer itself as some new and improved version of lesbian and gay but rather as something that questions the assumption that those descriptors are self-evident. Queer is not a conspiracy to discredit lesbian and gay; it does not seek to devalue the indisputable gains made in their name. Its principal achievement is to draw attention to the assumptions that—intentionally or otherwise—inhere in the mobilisation of any identity category, including itself.

9

Afterword

Almost as soon as queer established market dominance as a diacritical term, and certainly before consolidating itself in any easy vernacular sense, some theorists were already suggesting that its moment had passed and that 'queer politics may, by now, have outlived its political usefulness' (Halperin, 1995:112). Does queer become defunct the moment it is an intelligible and widely disseminated term? Teresa de Lauretis, the theorist often credited with inaugurating the phrase 'queer theory' (Wiegman, 1994:17), abandoned it barely three years later, on the grounds that it had been taken over by those mainstream forces and institutions it was coined to resist.

In 1991 de Lauretis edited a special issue of the journal *differences* under the subtitle *Queer Theory: Lesbian and Gay Sexualities*. In introducing it she describes the brief of the conference on lesbian and gay sexualities at which the papers collected in this issue were given: 'the project of the conference was based on the speculative premise that homosexuality is no longer to be seen simply as marginal with regard to a dominant, stable form of sexuality (heterosexuality) against which it would be defined either by opposition or homology' (de Lauretis, 1991:iii). Arguing that it is not productive to represent lesbian and gay sexualities either 'as merely transgressive or deviant vis-à-vis a proper, natural sexuality ... or as just another, optional "life-style"', de Lauretis wants them reconceptualised 'as social and cultural forms in their own right, albeit emergent ones and thus still fuzzily defined, undercoded, or discursively dependent on more established forms' (ibid.). She is especially interested in foregrounding the ways in which 'lesbian and gay'—as a naturalised rubric—itself delimits the theorisation of sexualities by emphasising or installing as unproblematic certain discourses, identities, communities and life-styles. Pointing to—among other things—race and gender bias in 'the discourse of white gay historiography and sociology', de Lauretis intends 'queer' to function as a critically disruptive term: 'juxtaposed to the "lesbian and gay" of the subtitle, [it] is intended to mark a certain critical distance from the latter, by now established and often convenient, formula' (ibid.:iv).

The essays published in de Lauretis's collection certainly work against those reified notions of sexual identity that she finds implicit in the phrase 'lesbian and gay'. Yet they rarely have recourse to the 'queer' terminology that de Lauretis offers as a discursive solution. They problematise the homogeneity of lesbian and gay identities with reference to such matters as race, the differences between medical and common-sense discourses of safe-sex practices and the psychoanalytic formulations of gender and sexuality but they do so overwhelmingly from within the categories of lesbian and gay. Three years after de Lauretis's volume, *differences* published a second queer issue, this time subtitled *More Gender Trouble: Feminism Meets Queer Theory*, with an introductory essay by Judith Butler. As may be expected, the term queer is used in this later volume by well over half of the contributors. Less expected—given de Lauretis's hope that queer might signify a new self-reflexivity, and attest to 'the necessary critical work of deconstructing our own discourses and their constructed silences' (ibid.)—is the fairly routine way in which that term is deployed, whether prefacing an essay or just being mentioned in passing. In other words, these essays often use 'queer' as a self-evident term of nomination in much the same way that 'lesbian and gay' has been deployed. Casual references to 'the impact of gay, lesbian, and queer theory' (Grosz, 1994b:274) and 'feminism and queer theory' (Hope, 1994:211) mark a recent terminological consolidation around queer which de Lauretis herself here acknowledges indirectly. Explaining her choice of terminology in

The Practice of Love: Lesbian Sexuality and Perverse Desire (1994),
de Lauretis (1994a:297) writes: 'As for "queer theory", my insistent
specification *lesbian* may well be taken as a taking of distance
from what, since I proposed it as a working hypothesis for lesbian
and gay studies in this very journal (*differences*, 3.2), has very
quickly become a conceptually vacuous creature of the publishing
industry'. Distancing herself from her earlier advocacy of queer, de
Lauretis now represents it as devoid of the political or critical
acumen she once thought it promised.

In some quarters and in some enunciations, no doubt, queer
does little more than function as shorthand for the unwieldy lesbian and gay, or offer itself as a new solidification of identity, by
kitting out more fashionably an otherwise unreconstructed sexual
essentialism. Certainly, 'its sudden and often uncritical adoption
has at times foreclosed what is potentially most significant—and
necessary—about the term' (Phillips, 1994:17). Queer retains,
however, a conceptually unique potential as a necessarily unfixed
site of engagement and contestation. Admittedly not discernible in
every mobilisation of queer, this constitutes an alternative to de
Lauretis's narrative of disillusionment. Judith Butler does not try to
anticipate exactly how queer will continue to challenge normative
structures and discourses. On the contrary, she argues that what
makes queer so efficacious is the way in which it understands the
effects of its interventions are not singular and therefore cannot be
anticipated in advance. Butler understands, as de Lauretis did
when initially promoting queer over lesbian and gay, that the conservative effects of identity classifications lie in their ability to
naturalise themselves as self-evident descriptive categories. She
argues that if queer is to avoid simply replicating the normative
claims of earlier lesbian and gay formations, it must be conceived
as a category in constant formation:

> [It] will have to remain that which is, in the present, never fully
> owned, but always and only redeployed, twisted, queered from
> a prior usage and in the direction of urgent and expanding
> political purposes, and perhaps also yielded in favor of terms
> that do that political work more effectively. (Butler, 1993:19)

In stressing the partial, flexible and responsive nature of queer,

Butler offers a corrective to those naturalised and seemingly self-evident categories of identification that constitute traditional formations of identity politics. She specifies the ways in which the logic of identity politics—which is to gather together similar subjects so that they can achieve shared aims by mobilising a minority-rights discourse—is far from natural or self-evident. Michael Warner (1993b:xvii) makes a similar point about the cultural specificity of identity politics when observing that, because its 'frame . . . belongs to Anglo-American traditions', it therefore 'has some distorting influences'.

In the sense that Butler outlines the queer project—that is, to the extent that she argues there can't be one—queer may be thought of as activating an identity politics so attuned to the constraining effects of naming, of delineating a foundational category which precedes and underwrites political intervention, that it may better be understood as promoting a non-identity—or even anti-identity—politics. If a potentially infinite coalition of sexual identities, practices, discourses and sites might be identified as queer, what it betokens is not so much liberal pluralism as a negotiation of the very concept of identity itself. For queer is, in part, a response to perceived limitations in the liberationist and identity-conscious politics of the gay and lesbian feminist movements. The rhetoric of both has been structured predominantly around self-recognition, community and shared identity; inevitably, if inadvertently, both movements have also resulted in exclusions, delegitimation, and a false sense of universality. The discursive proliferation of queer has been enabled in part by the knowledge that identities are fictitious—that is, produced by and productive of material effects but nevertheless arbitrary, contingent and ideologically motivated.

Unlike those identity categories labelled lesbian or gay, queer has developed out of the theorising of often unexamined constraints in traditional identity politics. Consequently, queer has been produced largely outside the registers of recognition, truthfulness and self-identity. For Butler (1993a:19), this is the democratising potential of queer:

> As much as identity terms must be used, as much as 'outness' is to be affirmed, these same notions must become subject to a

critique of the exclusionary operations of their own production: for whom is outness an historically available and affordable option? . . . Who is represented by *which* use of the term, and who is excluded? For whom does the term present an impossible conflict between racial, ethnic, or religious affiliation and sexual politics?

Queer, then, is an identity category that has no interest in consolidating or even stabilising itself. It maintains its critique of identity-focused movements by understanding that even the formation of its own coalitional and negotiated constituencies may well result in exclusionary and reifying effects far in excess of those intended.

Acknowledging the inevitable violence of identity politics and having no stake in its own hegemony, queer is less an identity than a *critique* of identity. But it is in no position to imagine itself outside that circuit of problems energised by identity politics. Instead of defending itself against those criticisms that its operations inevitably attract, queer allows such criticisms to shape its— for now unimaginable—future directions. 'The term', writes Butler (ibid.:20), 'will be revised, dispelled, rendered obsolete to the extent that it yields to the demands which resist the term precisely because of the exclusions by which it is mobilized'. The mobilisation of queer—*no less than the critique* of it—foregrounds the conditions of political representation: its intentions and effects, its resistance to and recovery by the existing networks of power.

For Halperin, as for Butler, queer is a way of pointing ahead without knowing for certain what to point at. '"Queer" . . . does not designate a class of already objectified pathologies or perversions', writes Halperin (1995:62); 'rather, it describes a horizon of possibility whose precise extent and heterogenous scope cannot in principle be delimited in advance'. Queer is always an identity under construction, a site of permanent becoming: 'utopic in its negativity, queer theory curves endlessly toward a realization that its realization remains impossible' (Edelman, 1995:346). The extent to which different theorists have emphasised the unknown potential of queer suggests that its most enabling characteristic may well be its potential for looking forward without anticipating the future. Instead of theorising queer in terms of its opposition to identity politics, it is more accurate to represent it as ceaselessly interrogating both the preconditions of identity and its effects. Queer is not outside the magnetic field of identity. Like some post-modern architecture, it turns identity inside out, and displays its supports exoskeletally. If the dialogue between queer and more traditional identity formations is sometimes fraught—which it is—that is not because they have nothing in common. Rather, lesbian and gay faith in the authenticity or even political efficacy of identity categories and the queer suspension of all such classifications energise each other, offering in the 1990s—and who can say beyond?—the ambivalent reassurance of an unimaginable future.

Notes

2 Theorising Same-Sex Desire

[1] Foucault's disregard for gender—or rather, the way in which the generic subject in his writings is ubiquitously masculine—has been frequently and soundly critiqued. Despite this limitation, many of Foucault's arguments have been taken up and expanded in recent feminist work: see, for example, Diamond and Quinby (1988). A Foucauldian study which has proved invigorating for a specifically lesbian theory is Judith Butler's *Gender Trouble* (1990).

[2] Heterosexuality has yet to be adequately theorised and much of the initial work completed to date has been undertaken by gay scholars. Henry Abelove has investigated the origins of heterosexuality (1992) and is currently completing a book whose title, *The Making of the Modern Heterosexual*, refers to Ken Plummer's classic, *The Making of the Modern Homosexual* (1981), while Jonathan Katz's *The Invention of Heterosexuality* (1996) makes clear in its title its debt to Foucault's account of the origins of homosexuality.

[3] North America is specified here because Australia has responded differently to the AIDS crisis, in part as a consequence of learning from the American example: 'Australia's response to HIV/AIDS has been characterised by a co-operative partnership between government and non-government sectors, and between policy makers, health professionals and the communities

most affected by HIV/AIDS' (Bartos, 1993:9). For an account of how British responses to the epidemic differed from American, see Derbyshire, 1994:41–2.

[4] There is something oxymoronic about the phrase 'premodern sexualities' in so far as the very notion of a sexuality—the reification of sexual practices as part of an individual's subject formation—in part constitutes the modern. Yet the phrase evidences both the necessity for and the difficulty of distinguishing between different historical understandings of sex and identity. Critics who problematise, rather than regard as axiomatic, the disjunction between premodern and modern sexual organisation include Jonathan Goldberg (1992) and Valerie Traub (1995).

3 The Homophile Movement

[1] The comparative mildness of the English homophile movement is often attributed to the paralysing effect of the scandalous trial and conviction of Oscar Wilde for 'gross indecency' in 1895. According to Cohen (1993:97–102), those trials 'play[ed] no small part in crystallizing the concept of "male homosexuality" in the Victorian sexual imagination'.

4 Gay Liberation

[1] Taking a slightly different perspective, John D'Emilio argues that the raid on Stonewall was resisted precisely because 'by 1969, bar raids were no longer commonplace in New York City' (1992b:240). D'Emilio points out that in the brief period in which successful homophile intervention and a liberal city administration had curbed police harassment, a sense of gay community had coalesced at such public places as bars. But when in the spring of 1969, under the demands of a mayoral campaign, police raids began again, there was now resistance to what had once been a standard occurrence.

5 Lesbian Feminism

[1] Fortunately for Atkinson, she is more often remembered for her

later and more affirmative assessment of lesbianism's relation to feminism: 'Feminism is the theory; lesbianism the practice' (ibid.:238).

2 Early gay male liberation discourse also referred to discrimination on the grounds of sexuality as 'sexism', analysing it overwhelmingly in terms of gender:

> sexism is a belief or practice that the sex or sexual orientation of human beings gives to some the right to certain privileges, powers, or roles, while denying to others their full potential. Within the context of our society, sexism is primarily manifested through male supremacy and heterosexual chauvinism (Young, 1992:7).

The term was also used in liberationist discourse to describe what might now be called 'sexual objectification' (Altman, 1973:17). It is used even more broadly in the Melbourne-based (but obviously American-inspired) 'Radicalesbian Manifesto': 'We see all oppression—capitalist/worker, white/black, imperialist/third world—as sexist, that is, as based on male power' (Radical Lesbians, 1973:8).

6 Limits of Identity

1 A similar although less widespread reaction to the rise of earlier gay liberatory identity categories has been noted by Marotta (1981:105–8): drag queens and butch lesbians were among those who felt disenfranchised by the domination of countercultural models of lesbian and gay identity.

7 Queer

1 David Halperin (1995:25–6) makes a careful argument about how Foucault's work relates to the priorities and practices of the new social movements. Rather than argue that the former simply inspires the latter, he suggests that Foucault's theorisation of power was a consequence of his knowledge and experience of those movements, and that many of his influential concepts circulated subsequently in more mediated circumstances.

8 Contestations of Queer

1 Queer, in this sense, has proved a useful category for scholars who seek to discuss sexuality outside the organising dichotomy of heterosexuality/homosexuality, such as Michael J. Sweet and Leonard Zwilling (1993:603), who translate the Sanskrit *klibatva* and *napumsakatva* as 'queerness' when discussing classical Indian medicine.

2 Activist approaches to this problem—namely, how to resist 'the erasure of lesbian sexuality'—are discussed by Anne Marie Smith (1992:200–13).

Bibliography

Abbott, Sidney and Barbara Love (1973) *Sappho Was A Right-On Woman: A Liberated View of Lesbianism*, New York: Stein and Day

Abelove, Henry (1992) 'Some Speculations on the History of "Sexual Intercourse" During the "Long Eighteenth Century" in England' in Andrew Parker et al. (eds) *Nationalisms and Sexualities*, New York: Routledge, pp. 335–42

—— (1993) 'From Thoreau to Queer Politics', *The Yale Journal of Criticism* 6, 2, pp. 17–27

Abelove, Henry et al. (eds) (1993) *The Lesbian and Gay Studies Reader*, New York: Routledge

Adam, Barry D. (1987) *The Rise of a Gay and Lesbian Movement*, Boston: Twayne

Alinder, Gary (1992) 'Gay Liberation Meets the Shrinks' in Jay and Young (eds) *Out of the Closets*, pp. 141–4

Allison, Dorothy (1984) 'Public Silence, Private Terror' in Vance (ed.) *Pleasure and Danger*, pp. 103–14

Altman, Dennis (1972) *Homosexual Oppression and Liberation*, Sydney: Angus and Robertson [1971]

—— (1973) 'What Is Sexism?', *Melbourne Gay Liberation Newsletter* 6, November–December, pp. 17–19

—— (1982) *The Homosexualization of America, The Americanization of the Homosexual*, New York: St Martin's Press

—— (1990) 'My America—and Yours: A Letter to US Lesbian and

Gay Activists', *Out/Look: National Lesbian and Gay Quarterly* 8, pp. 62–5

Angelides, Stephen (1994) 'The Queer Intervention', *Melbourne Journal of Politics* 22, pp. 66–88

Anon. (1974) 'Gay Rights Now: A Gay Manifesto', *National U,* 15 July, p. 5

Balka, Christine and Andy Rose (eds) (1989) *Twice Blessed: On Being Lesbian, Gay and Jewish,* Boston: Beacon Press

Barnard, Ian (1993) 'Queer Fictions: Gay Men with/and/in/near/or Lesbian Feminisms?', *Literature, Interpretation,* Theory 4, pp. 261–74

Barthes, Roland (1978) *Mythologies,* trans. Annette Lavers, New York: Hill and Wang [Fr 1957]

Bartos, Michael et al. (1993) *Meanings of Sex Between Men,* Canberra: Australian Government Publishing Service

Beam, Joseph (ed.) (1986) *In The Life,* Boston: Alyson

Bebbington, Laurie and Margaret Lyons (1975) 'Why Should We Work With You?: Lesbian-feminists Versus Gay Men', *Homosexual Conference Papers* (Melbourne), pp. 26–9

Berlant, Lauren and Elizabeth Freeman (1992) 'Queer Nationality', *Boundary 2* 19, pp. 149–80

Berlant, Lauren and Michael Warner (1995) 'What Does Queer Theory Teach Us About X?', *PMLA* 110, 3, pp. 343–9

Bersani, Leo (1995) *Homos,* Cambridge, Mass.: Harvard University Press

Bonwick, Philippa (1993) 'It is Cool to be Queer, but . . . '*Brother Sister* (Melbourne), 3 December, p. 10

Brasell, R. Bruce (1995) 'Queer Nationalism and the Musical Fag Bashing of John Greyson's *The Making of "Monsters"* ', *Wide Angle* 16, 3, pp. 26–36

Bray, Alan (1988) *Homosexuality in Renaissance England,* London: Gay Men's Press [1982]

Brett, Philip et al. (eds) (1994) *Queering the Pitch: The New Gay and Lesbian Musicology,* New York: Routledge

Bristow, Joseph and Angelia R. Wilson (eds) (1993) *Activating Theory: Lesbian, Gay and Bisexual Politics,* London: Lawrence and Wishart

Burston, Paul and Colin Richardson (eds) (1995) *A Queer Ro-*

mance: Lesbians, Gay Men and Popular Culture, London: Routledge

Butler, Judith (1990) *Gender Trouble: Feminism and the Subversion of Identity*, New York: Routledge

—— (1991) 'Imitation and Gender Insubordination' in Fuss (ed.) *Inside/Out*, pp. 13–31

—— (1993a) *Bodies That Matter: On the Discursive Limits of "Sex"*, New York: Routledge

—— (1993b) 'Critically Queer', *GLQ: A Journal of Lesbian and Gay Studies* 1, 1, pp. 17–32

—— (1994) 'Against Proper Objects', *differences: A Journal of Feminist Cultural Studies* 6, 2–3, pp. 1–26

Califia, Pat (1983) 'Gay Men, Lesbians, and Sex: Doing It Together', *Advocate*, 7 July, pp. 24–7

Carbery, Graham (1993) 'Camp to Queer', *Brother Sister* (Melbourne), 13 August, p. 9

Castle, Terry (1993) *The Apparitional Lesbian: Female Homosexuality and Modern Culture*, New York: Columbia University Press

Chauncey, George Jr (1982) 'From Sexual Inversion to Homosexuality: Medicine and the Changing Conceptualization of Female Deviance', *Salmagundi* 58–9, pp. 114–46

—— (1994) *Gay New York: Gender, Urban Culture, and the Making of the Gay Male World, 1890–1940*, New York: HarperCollins

Chee, Alexander (1991) 'A Queer Nationalism', *Out/Look: National Lesbian and Gay Quarterly* 11, pp. 15–19

Chicago Gay Liberation Front (1992) 'A Leaflet for the American Medical Association' in Jay and Young (eds) *Out of the Closets*, pp. 145–7

Chinn, Sarah E. and Kris Franklin (1993) 'The (Queer) Revolution Will Not Be Liberalised', *Minnesota Review* 40, pp. 138–50

Clausen, Jan (1990) 'My Interesting Condition', *Out/Look: National Lesbian and Gay Quarterly* 7, pp. 11–21

Cohen, Ed (1991) 'Who Are "We"? Gay "Identity" as Political (E)motion (A Theoretical Rumination)' in Fuss (ed.) *Inside/Out*, pp. 71–92

—— (1993) *Talk on the Wilde Side: Toward a Genealogy of a Discourse on Male Sexualities*, New York: Routledge

Cossen, Steve (1991) 'Queer', *Outlook: National Lesbian and Gay Quarterly* 11, pp. 20–3

Craft, Christopher (1989) '"Kiss Me With Those Red Lips": Gender and Inversion in Bram Stoker's *Dracula*' in Elaine Showalter (ed.) *Speaking of Gender*, New York: Routledge, Chapman and Hall, pp. 216–42

Creed, Barbara (1994) 'Queer Theory and Its Discontents: Queer Desires, Queer Cinema' in Norma Grieve and Ailsa Burns (eds) *Australian Women: Contemporary Feminist Thought*, Melbourne: Oxford University Press, pp. 151–64

Crimp, Douglas (1993) 'Right On, Girlfriend!' in Warner (ed.) *Fear of a Queer Planet*, pp. 300–20

Cruikshank, Margaret (ed.) (1982) *Lesbian Studies: Present and Future*, London: The Feminist Press

—— (1992) *The Gay and Lesbian Liberation Movement*, New York: Routledge

D'Arc, Johnny (1995) Queer Studies List, Monday, 6 February, 18:04

Däumer, Elizabeth D. (1992) 'Queer Ethics; or, The Challenge of Bisexuality to Lesbian Ethics', *Hypatia* 7, 4, pp. 91–105

Davidson, James (1994) 'It's Only Fashion', *London Review of Books*, 24 November, p. 12

de Lauretis, Teresa (1991) 'Queer Theory: Lesbian and Gay Sexualities', *differences: A Journal of Feminist Cultural Studies* 3, 2, pp. iii–xviii

—— (1994a) 'Habit Changes', *differences: A Journal of Feminist Cultural Studies* 6, 2–3, pp. 296–313

—— (1994b) *The Practice of Love: Lesbian Sexuality and Perverse Desire*, Bloomington: Indiana University Press

D'Emilio, John (1983) *Sexual Politics, Sexual Communities: The Making of a Homosexual Minority in the United States 1940–1970*, Chicago: University of Chicago Press

—— (1992a) 'Foreword' in Jay and Young (eds) *Out of the Closets*, pp. xi–xxix

—— (1992b) *Making Trouble: Essays on Gay History, Politics and the University*, New York: Routledge

Derbyshire, Philip (1995) 'A Measure of Queer', *Critical Quarterly* 36, 1, pp. 39–45

Diamond, Irene and Lee Quinby (eds) (1988) *Feminism and Foucault: Reflections on Resistance*, Boston: Northeastern University Press

Doan, Laura (ed.) (1994) *The Lesbian Postmodern*, New York: Columbia University Press

Doty, Alexander (1993) *Making Things Perfectly Queer: Interpreting Mass Culture*, Minneapolis: University of Minnesota Press

Dowsett, G. W. (1991) *Men Who Have Sex with Men: National HIV/AIDS Education*, Canberra: Australian Government Publishing Service

Duggan, Lisa (1992) 'Making It Perfectly Queer', *Socialist Review* 22, pp. 11–31

Dynes, Wayne R. (1990) *Encyclopedia of Homosexuality*, New York: Garland Publishing

Echols, Alice (1989) *Daring To Be Bad: Radical Feminism in America 1967–1975*, Minneapolis: University of Minnesota Press

Edelman, Lee (1994) *Homographesis: Essays in Gay Literary and Cultural Theory*, New York: Routledge

—— (1995) 'Queer Theory: Unstating Desire', *GLQ: A Journal of Lesbian and Gay Studies* 2, 4, pp. 343–6

Escoffier, Jeffrey (1990) 'Inside the Ivory Closet: The Challenges Facing Lesbian and Gay Studies', *Out/Look: National Lesbian and Gay Quarterly* 10, pp. 40–8

—— (1992) 'Generations and Paradigms: Mainstreams in Lesbian and Gay Studies' in Minton (ed.) *Gay and Lesbian Studies*, pp. 7–26

Faderman, Lillian (1985) *Surpassing the Love of Men: Romantic Friendship and Love Between Women from the Renaissance to the Present*, London: The Women's Press

Farwell, Marilyn (1992) untitled review of *Lesbian and Gay Writing: An Anthology of Critical Essays* and *The Safe Sea of Women: Lesbian Fiction, 1969–89, Journal of the History of Sexuality* 3, 1, pp. 165–7

Fenster, Mark (1993) 'Queer Punk Fanzines: Identity, Community, and the Articulation of Homosexuality and Hardcore', *Journal of Communication Inquiry* 17, 1, pp. 73–94

Ferguson, Ann et al. (1981) 'On "Compulsory Heterosexuality and

Lesbian Existence": Defining the Issues', *Signs: Journal of Women in Culture and Society* 7, 158–99

Foucault, Michel (1979) 'Truth and Power: Interview with Alessandro Fontano and Pasquale Pasquino' in *Michel Foucault: Power, Truth, Strategy*, trans. Paul Patton and Meaghan Morris, Sydney: Feral Publications, pp. 29–48

—— (1981) *The History of Sexuality, vol. 1, An Introduction* [1978], trans. Robert Hurley, Harmondsworth: Penguin [Fr 1976]

—— (1988a) 'Power and Sex', *Politics, Philosophy, Culture: Interviews and Other Writings, 1977–84*, trans. David J. Parent, ed. Lawrence D. Kritzman, New York: Routledge, pp. 110–24 [Fr 1977]

—— (1988b) 'What Is An Author?' in David Lodge (ed.) *Modern Criticism and Theory: A Reader*, London: Longman, pp. 197–210 [Fr 1969]

Friedan, Betty (1965) *The Feminine Mystique*, Harmondsworth: Penguin [1963]

Frye, Marilyn (1983) *The Politics of Reality: Essays in Feminist Theory*, New York, The Crossing Press

Fuss, Diana (1989) *Essentially Speaking: Feminism, Nature and Difference*, New York: Routledge

—— (ed.) (1991) *Inside/Out: Lesbian Theories, Gay Theories*, New York: Routledge

Galbraith, Larry (1993) 'Who Are We Now? The Gay vs Queer Debate', *Outrage*, July, pp. 22–5, 71

Garber, Marjorie (1995) *Vice Versa: Bisexuality and the Eroticism of Everyday Life*, New York: Simon and Schuster

Gates, Henry Louis (ed.) (1985) *'Race', Writing and Difference*, Chicago: University of Chicago Press

A Gay Male Group (1992) 'Notes on Gay Male Consciousness-Raising' in Jay and Young (eds) *Out of the Closets*, pp. 293–301

Gay Pride Week News (1973) 1, August

Gay Revolution Party Manifesto (1992) in Jay and Young (eds) *Out of the Closets*, pp. 342–5

Goldberg, Jonathan (1992) *Sodometries: Renaissance Texts, Modern Sexualities*, Stanford: Stanford University Press

Graham, Paula (1995) 'Girl's Camp? The Politics of Parody' in Tasmin Wilton (ed.) *Immortal, Invisible: Lesbians and the Moving Image*, London: Routledge, pp. 163–81

Grosz, Elizabeth (1994a) 'Experimental Desire: Rethinking Queer Subjectivity' in Joan Copjec (ed.) *Supposing the Subject*, London: Verso, pp. 133–57

—— (1994b) 'The Labors of Love: Analyzing Perverse Desire: An Interrogation of Teresa de Lauretis's *The Practice of Love', differences: A Journal of Feminist Cultural Studies* 6, 2–3, pp. 274–95

—— (1995) *Space, Time and Perversion: The Politics of Bodies*, Sydney: Allen and Unwin

Gurvich, Victoria (1995) 'Heterosexual Advertising Plan Angers AIDS Group', *Age* (Melbourne), 15 March, p. 2

Hall, Radclyffe (1968) *The Well of Loneliness*, London: Corgi Books [1928]

Hall, Stuart (1994) 'The Question of Cultural Identity' in *The Polity Reader in Cultural Theory*, Cambridge: Polity Press, pp. 119–25

Halberstam, Judith (1994) 'F2M: The Making of Female Masculinity' in Doan (ed.) *The Lesbian Postmodern*, pp. 210–28

Halperin, David (1990) 'Homosexuality: A Cultural Construct. An Exchange with Richard Schneider' in *One Hundred Years of Homosexuality and Other Essays on Greek Love*, New York: Routledge, pp. 41–53

—— (1995) *Saint Foucault: Towards a Gay Hagiography*, New York: Oxford University Press

Hanson, Ellis (1991) 'Undead' in Fuss (ed.) *Inside/Out*, pp. 324–40

—— (1993) 'Technology, Paranoia and the Queer Voice', *Screen* 34, 2, pp. 137–61

Haraway, Donna (1989) 'The Biopolitics of Postmodern Bodies: Determinations of Self in Immune System Discourses', *differences: A Journal of Feminist Cultural Studies* 1, 1, pp. 3–43

Hawkins, Peter (1975) 'Effeminism', *Homosexual Conference Papers* (Melbourne), pp. 23–5

Hayes, Susan (1994) 'Coming Over All Queer', *New Statesman and Society*, 16 September, pp. 14–15

Hennessy, Rosemary (1993) 'Queer Theory: A Review of the

differences Special Issue and Wittig's *The Straight Mind'*, *Signs: Journal of Women in Culture and Society* 18, pp. 964–73

—— (1994) 'Queer Theory, Left Politics', *Rethinking Marxism* 7, 3, pp. 85–111

Herkt, David (1995) 'Being Gay', *RePublica*, 3, pp. 36–50

Hocquenghem, Guy (1993) *Homosexual Desire*, Durham: Duke University Press [1972]

Hodges, Lucy (1994) 'Queen of "Queer" Courts Controversy', *Australian*, 29 June, p. 27

Hope, Trevor (1994) 'The "Returns" of Cartography: Mapping Identity-In(-)Difference', *differences: A Journal of Feminist Cultural Studies*, 6, 2–3, pp. 208–11

Hurley, Michael and Craig Johnston (1975) 'Campfires of the Resistance: Theory and Practice for the Liberation of Male Homosexuals', *Homosexual Conference Papers* (Melbourne), pp. 24–9

Hutchins, Loraine and Lani Kaahumanu (eds) (1991) *Bi Any Other Name: Bisexual People Speak Out*, Boston: Alyson

Irigaray, Luce (1981) 'When the Goods Get Together' in Elaine Marks and Isabelle de Courtivron (eds) *New French Feminisms*, New York: Schocken, pp. 107–11 [Fr 1977]

Jackson, Earl Jr (1995) *Strategies of Deviance: Studies in Gay Male Representation*, Bloomington: Indiana University Press

Jagose, Annamarie (1994) *Lesbian Utopics*, New York: Routledge

Jay, Karla and Allen Young (eds) (1992) *Out of the Closets: Voices of Gay Liberation*, London: Gay Men's Press [1972]

Jeff (1972) 'Aversion Therapy', *Gay Rays* (Melbourne), December, p. 7

Jeffreys, Sheila (1993) *The Lesbian Heresy: A Feminist Perspective on the Lesbian Sexual Revolution*, Melbourne: Spinifex Press

—— (1994) 'The Queer Disappearance of Lesbians: Sexuality in the Academy' *Women's Studies International Forum* 17, 5, pp. 459–72

Johnston, Jill (1973) *Lesbian Nation: The Feminist Solution*, New York: Simon and Schuster

Jones, Stephen (1992) 'Queerer than Fuck!', *Outrage*, November, pp. 26–8

Kahey, Regina (1976) 'A Good Gay History Bursts Out of the Closet', *Village Voice*, 6 December, p. 94

Katz, Jonathan (1976) *Gay American History: Lesbians and Gay Men in the U.S.A.*, New York: Thomas Cromwell

——— (1983) *Gay/Lesbian Almanac: A New Documentary*, New York: Harper and Row

——— (1996) *The Invention of Heterosexuality*, New York: Penguin

Kamp, David (1993) 'The Straight Queer', *GQ*, July, pp. 95–9

Koestenbaum, Wayne (1993) 'Excess Story' *Village Voice Literary Supplement*, October, p. 18

Lauritsen, John and David Thorstad (1974) *The Early Homosexual Rights Movement*, New York: Times Change Press

Leng, Kwok Wei and Kaz Ross (1994) 'Theorising Corporeality: Bodies, Sexuality and the Feminist Academy [interview with Elizabeth Grosz]', *Melbourne Journal of Politics* 22, pp. 3–29

Link, David (1993) 'I Am Not Queer', *Reason* 25, 4, pp. 45–9

McIntosh, Mary (1992) 'The Homosexual Role' in Stein (ed.) *Forms of Desire*, pp. 25–42

Maggenti, Maria (1991) 'Women As Queer Nationals', *Out/Look: National Lesbian and Gay Quarterly* 11, pp. 20–3

Malinowitz, Harriet (1993) 'Queer Theory: Whose Theory?', *Frontiers* 13, pp. 168–84

Marotta, Toby (1981) *The Politics of Homosexuality*, Boston: Houghton Mifflin

Martin, Biddy (1994a) 'Extraordinary Homosexuals and the Fear of Being Ordinary', *differences: A Journal of Feminist Cultural Studies* 6, 2–3, pp. 100–25

——— (1994b) 'Sexualities Without Genders and Other Queer Utopias', *Diacritics* 24, 2–3, pp. 104–21

Merck, Mandy (1993) *Perversions: Deviant Readings*, London: Virago Press

Meyer, Richard (1991) 'Rock Hudson's Body' in Fuss (ed.) *Inside/Out*, pp. 259–88

Minton, Henry L. (ed.) (1992) *Gay and Lesbian Studies*, New York: Haworth Press

Moraga, Cherríe and Gloria Anzaldúa (eds) (1983) *This Bridge Called My Back: Writings by Radical Women of Color*, New York: Kitchen Table Press

Morton, Donald (1993a) 'The Politics of Queer Theory in the (Post)-Modern Moment', *Genders* 17, Fall, pp. 121–50

—— (1993b) '"Radicalism", "Outing", and the Politics of (Sexual) Knowledges', *Minnesota Review* 40, pp. 151–6

—— (1995) 'Birth of the Cyberqueer', *PMLA* 110, 3, pp. 369–81

Nestle, Joan (1984) 'The Fem Question' in Vance (ed.) *Pleasure and Danger*, pp. 232–41

—— (1988) *A Restricted Country: Essays and Short Stories*, London: Sheba Feminist Press [1987]

Newton, Esther and Shirley Walton (1984) 'The Misunderstanding: Toward A More Precise Sexual Vocabulary' in Vance (ed.) *Pleasure and Danger*, pp. 242–50

Norton, Rictor (1992) *Mother Clap's Molly House: The Gay Subculture in England 1700–1830*, London: Gay Men's Press

Nunokawa, Jeff (1991) '"All the Sad Young Men": AIDS and the Work of Mourning' in Fuss (ed.) *Inside/Out*, pp. 311–23

O'Sullivan, Sue and Pratibha Parmar (1989) *Lesbians Talk Safer Sex*, London: Scarlet Press

Palmer, Paulina (1993) *Contemporary Lesbian Writing: Dreams, Desire, Difference*, Buckingham: Open University Press

Paris, Sherri (1993) untitled review of *A Lure of Knowledge: Lesbian Sexuality and Theory* and *Inside/Out: Lesbian Theories, Gay Theories, Signs: A Journal of Women in Culture and Society* 18, 4, pp. 984–8

Parnaby, Julia (1993) 'Queer Straits', *Trouble and Strife* 26, pp. 13–16

Phillips, David (1994) 'What's So Queer Here? Photography at the Gay and Lesbian Mardi Gras', *Eyeline* 26, pp. 16–19

Plummer, Ken (ed.) (1981) *The Making of the Modern Homosexual*, London: Hutchinson

Powers, Ann (1993) 'Queer in the Streets, Straight in the Sheets: Notes on Passing', *Utne Reader*, Nov./Dec., pp. 74–80

Radical Lesbians (1973) 'The Radicalesbians Manifesto', *Melbourne Gay Liberation Newsletter*, September, pp. 8–9

Reed, Christopher (1993) '"Queer" a Sneer no more', *Age*, 30 June, p. 15

Rich, Adrienne (1986) *Blood, Bread and Poetry: Selected Prose, 1979–1985*, New York, W. W. Norton

Riley, Denise (1988) *Am I That Name? Feminism and the Category of 'Women' in History*, Minneapolis: University of Minnesota Press

Rubin, Gayle (1981) 'The Leather Menace', in Samois (ed.) *Coming to Power: Writings and Graphics on Lesbian S/M*, Berkeley: Samois, pp. 194–229

—— (1993) 'Thinking Sex' in Abelove et al. (eds) *The Lesbian and Gay Studies Reader*, pp. 3–44

Saalfield, Catherine and Ray Navarro (1991) 'Shocking Pink Praxis: Race and Gender on the ACT UP Frontlines' in Fuss (ed.) *Inside/Out*, pp. 341–69

Schneir, Miriam (ed. and intros) (1994) *Feminism in Our Time: The Essential Writings, World War II to the Present*, New York: Vintage Books

Schramm-Evans, Zoë (1993) 'Internal Politics', *Body Politic* 4, pp. 39–41

Schwichtenberg, Cathy (ed.) (1993) *The Madonna Connection: Representational Politics, Subcultural Identities, and Cultural Theory*, Sydney: Allen and Unwin

Sedgwick, Eve Kosofsky (1990) *Epistemology of the Closet*, Berkeley: University of California Press

—— (1992) *Between Men: English Literature and Male Homosocial Desire*, New York: Columbia University Press [1985]

—— (1993a) *Tendencies*, Durham: Duke University Press

—— (1993b) 'Queer Performativity: Henry James's *The Art of the Novel*', *GLQ: A Journal of Lesbian and Gay Studies* 1, 1, pp. 1–16

Seidman, Steven (1993) 'Identity and Politics in a "Postmodern" Gay Culture: Some Historical and Conceptual Notes' in Warner (ed.) *Fear of a Queer Planet*, pp. 105–42

—— (1994) 'Symposium: Queer Theory/Sociology: A Dialogue', *Sociological Theory* 12, 2, pp. 166–77

Shelley, Martha (1992) 'Gay Is Good' in Jay and Young (eds) *Out of the Closets*, pp. 31–4

Smith, Anne Marie (1992) 'Resisting the Erasure of Lesbian Sexuality: A Challenge to Queer Activism' in Ken Plummer (ed.) *Modern Homosexualities: Fragments of Lesbian and Gay Experience*, London: Routledge, pp. 200–13

Smith, Barbara (1993) 'Where's the Revolution?', *Nation*, 5 July, pp. 12–16

Smyth, Cherry (1992) *Lesbians Talk Queer Notions*, London: Scarlet Press

Stein, Arlene (1991) 'Sisters and Queers: The Decentering of Lesbian Feminism', *Socialist Review* 20, pp. 33–55

Stein, Edward (ed.) (1992a) *Forms of Desire: Sexual Orientation and the Social Constructionist Controversy*, New York: Routledge

Stein, Edward (1992b) 'Conclusion: The Essentials of Constructionism and the Construction of Essentialism' in Stein (ed.) *Forms of Desire*, pp. 325–53

Sweet, Michael J. and Leonard Zwilling (1993) 'The First Medicalization: The Taxonomy and Etiology of Queerness in Classical Indian Medicine', *Journal of the History of Sexuality* 3, pp. 590–607

Third World Gay Revolution (Chicago) and Gay Liberation Front (Chicago) (1992) 'Gay Revolution and Sex Roles' in Jay and Young (eds) *Out of the Closets*, pp. 252–9

Thomas, Keith (1980) 'Rescuing Homosexual History' *New York Review of Books*, 4 July, pp. 26–9

Thompson, Denise (1985) *Flaws in the Social Fabric: Homosexuals and Society in Sydney*, Sydney: George Allen and Unwin

Traub, Valerie (1995) 'The Psychomorphology of the Clitoris', *GLQ: A Journal of Lesbian and Gay Studies* 2, 1–2, pp. 81–113

Trebay, Guy (1990) 'In Your Face', *Village Voice*, August 14, pp. 34–9

Troubridge, Una (1973) *The Life of Radclyffe Hall*, New York: Citadel, New York [1963]

Vaid, Urvashi (1995) *Virtual Equality: The Mainstreaming of Lesbian and Gay Liberation*, New York: Anchor Books

Vance, Carol (ed.) (1984) *Pleasure and Danger: Exploring Female Sexuality*, Boston: Routledge and Kegan Paul

Warner, Michael (1992) 'From Queer to Eternity: An Army of Theorists Cannot Fail', *Village Voice Literary Supplement*, June, pp. 18–19

—— (1993a) *Fear of a Queer Planet: Queer Politics and Social Theory*, Minneapolis: University of Minnesota Press

—— (1993b) 'Introduction' in Warner (ed.) *Fear of a Queer Planet*, pp. vii–xxxi

Watney, Simon (1991) 'School's Out' in Fuss (ed.) *Inside/Out*, pp. 387–401
—— (1992) 'Homosexual, Gay or Queer? Activism, Outing and the Politics of Sexual Identities', *Outrage*, April, pp. 18–22
Watson, Lex (1974) 'The Patient as Victim', *Gay Liberation Press* (Sydney) 4, October, pp. 23–32
Weedon, Chris (1987) *Feminist Practice and Poststructuralist Theory*, Oxford: Basil Blackwell
Weeks, Jeffrey (1977) *Coming Out: Homosexual Politics in Britain from the Nineteenth Century to the Present*, London: Quartet Books
—— (1985) *Sexuality and Its Discontents: Meanings, Myths and Modern Sexualities*, London: Routledge and Kegan Paul
Weston, Kath (1993) 'Do Clothes Make the Woman?: Gender, Performance Theory, and Lesbian Eroticism', *Genders* 17, pp. 1–21
Wiegman, Robyn (1994) 'Introduction: Mapping the Lesbian Postmodern' in Doan (ed.), *The Lesbian Postmodern*, pp. 1–20
Wills, Sue (1972) 'Intellectual Poofter Bashers', *Camp Ink* 2, 11, pp. 4–11
Wittig, Monique (1992) *The Straight Mind and Other Essays*, Boston: Beacon
Wittman, Carl (1992) 'A Gay Manifesto' in Jay and Young (eds) *Out of the Closets*, pp. 330–42
Wolfe, Susan J. and Julia Penelope (eds) (1993) *Sexual Practice, Textual Theory: Lesbian Cultural Criticism*, Cambridge, Mass.: Blackwell
Wotherspoon, Garry (1991) *'City of the Plain': History of a Gay Sub-Culture*, Sydney: Hale and Iremonger
Yingling, Thomas (1991) 'AIDS in America: Postmodern Governance, Identity, and Experience' in Fuss (ed.) *Inside/Out*, pp. 291–310
Young, Allen (1992) 'Out of the Closets, Into the Streets' in Jay and Young (eds) *Out of the Closets*, pp. 6–31
Zimmerman, Bonnie (1995) 'From Lesbian Nation to Queer Nation', interview with Susan Sayer, *Hecate* 21, 2, pp. 29–43

Index